A MANUAL FOR
PROFESSIONAL ORGANIZERS

D1373072

By Cyndi Seidler

4th Edition

Banter Books

8209 Foothill Blvd. A184
Sunland, CA 91040

A MANUAL FOR PROFESSIONAL ORGANIZERS
Fourth Edition

Copyright © 1995, 1997, 2001, 2004 Cyndi Seidler

Published in the United States by
Banter Books
8209 Foothill Blvd. A184
Sunland, CA 91040

First Edition 1995.
Second Edition 1997, revised.
Third Edition 2001, revised.
Fourth Edition 2004, revised.

Publisher's Cataloging-in-Publication
　Seidler, Cyndi -- 4th ed.
　　1.　Careers　2.　Education　3. Business start-ups　I.　Title: A Manual for Professional
　　Organizers

ISBN 0-9705125-0-3
Library of Congress Control Number: 2004093846

Letter from Author

Dear colleague:

It is so gratifying to me to help aspiring organizers start their new business and career endeavor.

An organizing career is a very rewarding field. Working with clients to help them become better organized has many mutual satisfactions. You'll discover for yourself the wonderful feeling of helping someone improve conditions as you help shape their life into a more orderly state.

The information in this manual is provided as a guideline to starting up and running your own professional organizing business. It is based on my own research, findings and personal experience. Veteran organizers may also find this helpful in providing ideas to take their business to another level.

In this book, you'll learn out how to take your organizing skills and turn them into organizing services. You'll find out how to operate your organizing business and become a "business owner." After you see how easy it is to start and run your business, you'll learn some tactics on how to market it.

I wish you success and the kind of rewards this career has given me. I'm available for consultation or coaching and would enjoy the opportunity of assisting you further in your new business venture, so please feel free to get in touch with me.

For consultation arrangements, please contact me by email: cyndi@professional-organizers.com.

Sincerely,

Cyndi Seidler

P.S. Be sure to check out our training program at:
www.professional-organizers.com

Acknowledgements

I'd like to express my appreciation to all those who supported my career, giving me the vigor to go where I once only dreamed I could go.

I'd also like to thank my daughter, Heather, who has always given me the "high-five" hand-smack whenever I shared my successes with her.

Also, to NAPO for its ongoing support and education, and it's contributions to the organizing profession.

What lies behind us and what lies before us are small matters compared to what lies within us.
-- Ralph Waldo Emerson

Table of CONTENTS

ORGANIZING YOUR CLIENT

MARKETING & PROMOTING YOUR BUSINESS

INDUSTRY OVERVIEW

The Organizing Industry

U.S. News and World Report lists professional organizers as one of the Best Jobs for the Future.

The Need for Professional Services

Organization is essential to keeping any home or office running smoothly.

The explosive growth of the professional organizing industry has proven to be a great resource for individuals to get the organizing assistance they need.

For many years, people have struggled without the professional assistance needed to help them get organized. As a result, they suffered with clutter issues, inadequate filing systems, lost productivity, inefficiency, and general overwhelm.

Without the knowledge to create organizing systems, they have become victims of disorganization.

The condition of the industry today is such that professional organizers are needed now more than ever. Company downsizing and layoffs have been a major reason that many individuals have started home-based businesses, putting them in a situation of running things by themselves. They usually find they need experts to help them run their operations and are outsourcing to specialized professionals, including professional organizers.

Corporations need experts to consult on operations and management. As behind-the-scenes decision makers, these individuals influence private business decisions. Jobs once performed by corporate staff members are now outsourced to a pool of outside consultants. And the increasing complexity of doing business (especially with technological advancements) requires businesses to seek the advice of experts they cannot afford to keep on staff.

Individuals at home need experts to help them cope and maintain organization in the home because they lead busy lives and have become overwhelmed. Many people have moved from the office to working from home or forming home businesses. While they may be competent delivering the services they provide, they often do not know how to manage work, paper or information.

> *"Time-saving services like professional organizing are one of the fastest growing areas for home businesses."* - U.S. News 1998 Career Guide, 20 Hot Job Tracks.

Types of Professional Services

Some of the more predominant professional services in use have been consultants in the field of business, finance, marketing, and public relations.

The growth of organizing consultants indicates the further development of entrepreneurial expansion, having found its own niche in the service marketplace, both business and personal.

Industry Analysis

The demand for professional organizing services has been on a rise since the early 90's. The market for these services shows a 40% growth over the past two years.

Some of the reasons for the growth of the professional organizing industry include:

- The home office market has been growing at a rapid rate.
- Corporate down-sizing, with many people starting home businesses.
- Large volume of paperwork.
- Rise of reported cases of ADD/ADHD.
- Growth of paper produced each year.
- Increase of entrepreneurial expansion.
- Professionals starting businesses without business knowledge of running one.
- More media featuring professional organizers, both in print and television.

The industry is yours!

- 85-90% of documents once filed are NEVER retrieved. *(Survey conducted by Document Managers)*

- 50% of all filed material is duplicated or over-aged. *(Survey conducted by Document Managers)*

- The average U.S. executive spends up to 6 weeks each year searching or misplaced, misfiled, or mislabeled paperwork. *(Wall Street Journal)*

- The average professional loses one hour per day due to disorganization. *(Survey conducted by Video Arts and Training Net, 1997)*

- The average American will spend one year searching through desk clutter looking for misplaced objects. *(Margin, Dr. Richard Swenson)*

- Americans spend 1.3 billion hours a year preparing tax information. *(Forbes, 10/2000)*

- 81% of people consider themselves organized, yet 83% say getting MORE organized is among their goals. *(Scientific Survey, USA Weekend, 1998)*

About NAPO

What Is NAPO?

The National Association of Professional Organizers (NAPO) was established in 1985. It is a non-profit professional association whose members include organizing consultants, speakers, trainers, authors, and manufactures of organizing products.

NAPO's purpose is threefold:

1. To promote the profession of organizing.

2. To educate the public about the field of professional organizing.

3. To provide support, education, and a networking forum for the membership.

People doing business in the field of organizing include anything from time or information management to planning and organizing environments, to productivity or service improvement.

Joining NAPO makes you a member of the only national organization dedicated to promoting and supporting the field of professional organizing. For information, visit their Web site at www.napo.net.

BUSINESS OF
PROFESSIONAL ORGANIZING

What Is A Professional Organizer?

Professional organizers spawned out of the need to help people get better organized. This demand has grown exponentially since 1985, when the National Association of Professional Organizers (NAPO) was founded.

A professional organizer is defined by NAPO as:

People who provide information, products and assistance to help others get organized.

NAPO also states, "A professional organizer can provide ideas, information, structure, solutions, and systems which could increase productivity, reduce stress, and lead to more control over time, space, and activities."

The Role of Professional Organizers

Professional organizers play an important role in today's society. The reasons that individuals hire professional organizers are many, and your role may be different from another person's role -- depending on the job project or task function.

The role might be:

- Providing companies the means for business outsourcing to minimize payroll overhead expenses.
- Giving assistance for over-worked, overwhelmed, busy executives.
- Assisting people with their record-keeping.
- Helping people who can't manage time.
- Turning people's disorder into order.
- Handling the environment for people with organizational disorders.
- Offering solutions for those with organizational challenges.
- Providing assistance for those who have specialized needs.

Professional Organizers can be referred to by various "titles." These include:

Organizing consultant
Organization consultant
Organization Management consultant

Depending on the circumstances (i.e., doing a corporate project), you may choose a temporary title that fits a particular image for a specific job.

Benefits of a Professional Organizer

Client Goals and Objectives

As already mentioned, most of us are not "born" organized. It is something we learn and practice.

Achieving success in any area comes from applying a strategy to get from one place to another and from calculating our moves toward the attainment of our aim of getting there.

This applies to clients who need professional help in getting better organized. Some of their goals and objectives might include to:

- ✓ Exist in a clutter-free, "happy" environment
- ✓ Function with total efficiency
- ✓ Accomplish more in less time
- ✓ Balance time for work and personal life
- ✓ Work smarter, not harder

In isolating a client's purpose for getting organized, an organizer will be able to ascertain the best way, the "how" to help them. Here are some typical reasons a person wants to be organized:

- Focus better
- Be less stressed
- Be more efficient
- Be more productive
- Get things done
- Have more ease and convenience
- Be in control of their life

Practical solutions will flow once you understand the reason, the "why" they want to be organized.

Let your client realize that organizing is a process -- it is not an event. It's a way of adding simplicity to a life that seems complex.

Traits of a Business Owner

Professionalism

Having the right attitude and determination plays an important role in running your business. It starts by assuming the role of owner.

An organizer may not be wearing a suit on an organizing project (especially if they expect to end up on the floor sorting whatever!) however they need to present themselves professionally. It's a demeanor, a way of conducting ourselves and our business affairs.

Professionalism involves:

- Following through on all appointments and agreements, whether in writing or verbal

- Treating clients with respect

- Doing your best work and delivering on the expectations of the client

- Cooperating with business associates, clients, and people you're working with

- Keeping informed about your field

- Maintaining integrity

Confidence

Success in a business comes about from being confident in your ability to accomplish what you set out to do. Your confidence, combined with your abilities, will enable you to tackle most anything with determination.

When an organizer walks into a meeting or job appointment, an attitude of "owning the room" should be projected. This also makes the client feel safe in your hands and more apt to communicate to you freely and openly, as well as show you all those embarrassing or hidden disasters they need you to fix.

A client who is relaxed having you in their space won't be bothered by the fact you're opening drawers and cabinets in their areas to see what's lurking inside.

Persistence

Develop a positive attitude and you'll be able to discover solutions and deal more effectively if trouble strikes. By adapting persistence and a "stick-to-it-ness," you'll be able to survive many difficult situations.

While it may seem easier to give up on a given course, the true challenge is moving through obstacles and staying on track toward your goal.

View obstacles as a game and, instead of focusing on a bad situation, focus on creating solutions. Whatever your attention is on will determine your results.

Determination

While it's one thing to be persistent on something you're doing, it is another thing to have the determinism to accomplish it. That's why when you embark on any undertaking, you need a goal and the determination to reach that goal.

A person setting out to start a new business venture may be all fired up and eager to dive in, but without determination to arrive somewhere, they can become lost or fall off the tracks and drift in another direction.

As you wouldn't start a long trip to a place you haven't been before without a map, you wouldn't want to start a business without a map either. Therefore, mapping your route to a particular place helps feed your determination to stay on a given course.

PRACTICAL I-1:

Take a look at your traits and write a short essay that describes how your professionalism and attitude will reflect on your success. Note any traits you need to develop or improve on, if any.

Organizing Skills & Specialties

Organizing consultants vary in expertise, yet most have one thing in common - their ability to put order into disorder. Whether it is business or personal organizing, this common denominator must exist.

It isn't necessarily a factor that a person should naturally possess inherit organizing abilities. This is something which can be learned and individuals can learn by observation, study (specialized education in an area or subject) and/or with hands-on experience. All three elements combined work best.

Whether you want to specialize in business or personal organizing, an organizer should know the essential ingredients for either:

1) how to manage paper
2) how to manage time
3) how to manage information, or
4) how to manage a project

With the exception of a very specialized organizing service, those systems are most commonly utilized in this industry.

While there are many forms of organizing, by looking over the types of organizing areas which exist, one can fit their skills into providing one or more services.

The idea is to determine what your skills are and match your skills with a service or services. After that, continue to improve and expand your skills to deliver better quality and a wider range of service.

Value-added Services

As you grow your business and expand your expertise and knowledge, there are various opportunities that provide further growth development.

Partnering up in strategic alliances with product companies or businesses that compliment your services will increase your potential income base. Research the industry and determine what is best for you.

The field of organizing is only limited by one's skills or areas of expertise, which can be expanded upon through more education, knowledge and experience.

Skills List

General:

    Time Management
    Paper Management
    Clutter Management

Home:

Home organizing	OrganizingAttics/Basements
Home staging	Filing systems - home
Organizing closets, kitchens, garages	Collections, memorabilia, photos Household Management

Business:

Office organizing	Tracking Systems
File Management	Contact Management
Filing systems - business	Work Management

Personal:

Errands & shopping	Personal assistance
Wardrobe consulting	Research
Organizing travel	

Specialties:

Ergonomics	Organizing Charts/Boards
Space-planning	Business Planning & Development
Interior Design	Relocations
Closet Design	Finance
Garage Systems	Coaching
Storage Systems	Computer organizing
Disaster Preparedness	Estate Sales & Organizing
Records & Information Management	Event Organizing
Project Management	Photo & Asset Inventory
Policies & Procedures	ADD/ADHD consulting
	Feng Shui

PRACTICAL I-2:

1) List all your skills, both business and personal abilities. Circle all the ones you enjoy the most.

2) List all the services you feel comfortable in delivering. Circle all the ones you do the best.

Organization Technology

As an art, organization can evolve as a creative process. With organization technology, we're looking at the concept of applying creative methods and raw materials to create order.

Organization is not necessarily recognized as an art or a science or as a subject or an industry. Yet, it is all of the above. As there are rules and policies that govern our lives, there are guidelines to structure our lives. These guidelines are the basis of being able to function in any activity.

When we think of technology, we think of the application of scientific methods and materials used. With organization technology, we're looking at the concept of applying methods and materials to create order.

The principles of organization might, for example, carry the assumption that, in order to create an orderly space, there would have to be a place for everything and everything in its place.

So, creating an orderly environment, even if that environment is as small as a single drawer, certain materials might be necessary (like a drawer organizer).

As an art, organization can evolve as a creative process. Here, we might use our originality to come up with an imaginative approach to solving the problem of how to store shoes in an over-crowded closet. Or, it could be finding some interesting items and gadgets to stop clutter from piling up on a desk.

In using our originality, we can come up with an imaginative approach to solving organization problems.

Combine technology and art and you'll get solutions.

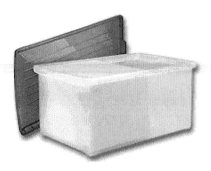

Professional Development ⇐

Business Coaches

Business coaches help bring out the best in you. They help in bringing a new perspective to a company's plans and activities and can be a valuable team player in the development and growth of a business.

A coach can act as a "sounding board" when we are working on creating new strategies or formulating a plan of action for a new or existing project. They can help provide guidance, find creative alternatives to business challenges, help in making choices, and embody the values and standards you live up to.

Continued Education

In order to improve and/or expand your area of expertise, it is important to attend workshops, seminars, and conventions which relate to business development, marketing, and your trade.

It is equally important to read and study material relating to the above. There are many books and magazines which help enhance our businesses and you only need to visit a bookstore or library to find information on the subjects you want.

CPO

The National Association of Professional Organizers (NAPO) has a Certification Program for Professional Organizers accredited by NCCA (National Commission for Certifying Agencies). This gives one the credentials of being a "Certified Professional Organizer" (C.P.O.). With this, one can show their credibility with the initials, C.P.O. after their name.

This is a voluntary certification available to the public, whether NAPO members or not. Certification is related to the education of the applicant and education is determined by various scales.

PRACTICAL I-3.

Observe what organizing books and tools are out there to stay educated and informed. Go to a bookstore to see what books are on the shelves relating to your trade so you can plan to stock your library.

Contractor Status

There are employment laws we should be aware of so we can protect ourselves when contracted with others.

A publication called "Independent Contractor Guidelines" by Thomas S. Pavone, Jr., Attorney At Law is a guide which is meant "to assist in a general understanding of the current law relating to employment matters. It is not to be regarded as legal advice."

- The contractor is not required to follow instructions on how to accomplish their job.
- The contractor does not receive training and uses their own methods to accomplish their work.
- The contractor has the right to hire others to do the job.
- The contractor that the work is not essential to the hiring firm.
- The contractor sets their own hours.
- The contractor doesn't have a continuing relationship with the hiring firm.
- Any assistants the contractor uses is at the sole discretion and supervision of the contractor.
- The contractor has time to pursue other gainful work.
- The contractor controls where they work.
- The contractor determines the order and sequence that they will perform the work.
- The contractor is not asked for progress or interim reports.
- The contractor works for more than one firm at a time.
- The contractor is responsible for their incidental expenses.
- The contractor furnishes their own tools.
- The contractor can perform their services without the hiring firm's facilities (equipment, furniture, machinery, etc.).
- The contractor makes their services available to the general public.
- The contractor can make a profit or a loss.
- The contractor can't be fired so long as they produce a result which meets the contract specifications.
- The contractor is responsible for the satisfactory completion of the job and is legally obligated to compensate the hiring firm for failure to complete.

Code of Conduct

I have written a code for professional organizers as a guideline toward professional conduct. *NOTE: This is not an endorsed code put out by NAPO. There is a "Code of Ethics" published by NAPO, available at napo.net.*

Code For Professional Organizers

1. To use all my skills and knowledge of organizing to the best of my ability to help my clients.

2. To be a role model in the field of organizing and do my best to display the kind of competence and professionalism in which upholds honor in the organizing industry.

3. To represent my services honestly and accurately.

4. To maintain integrity in my work and not accept any task in which I feel would not bring about the desired results that I set out to achieve.

5. To treat my clients with courtesy and try my best to generate goodwill.

6. To refuse to accept work from anyone I feel I am not qualified to help and try to help by suggesting the services of other qualified organizers in those areas which I cannot do.

7. To make every effort to keep all appointments made and be on time for all appointments scheduled.

8. To seek higher levels of knowledge, competence, and skill that will bring about further improvement in my profession.

9. To always represent myself in a professional and skilled manner.

10. To advocate trust and sustain confidentiality with any confidential client information.

11. To try my best to generate incentive for others to be organized.

GETTING STARTED

No

Start-up Costs

There are many books on the subject of starting-up a business and this chapter is not a crash course on it, although it will provide specific information and some useful guidelines to get a person up and going as a professional organizer.

Whether a person is starting out part-time or full-time, start-up costs can be relatively low. For the cost of a DBA ("Doing Business As"), some business cards, placing a classified ad or mailing out flyers, a professional organizer can commence business on a shoe-string budget under $200.00. Other expenses can follow, as a person's budget allows.

Preparing a start-up cost sheet will allow a person to see what expenses are needed. An example of this might include:

DBA	80.00
*Business license	0.00
Business insurance (down)	200.00
Business phone lines	100.00
Business cards and stationary	100.00
NAPO membership fees	200.00
Legal & Accounting fees	100.00
Advertising	200.00
Office supplies & materials	75.00
Office equipment	1500.00
PO Box	45.00
Web site domain & hosting set up fees (optional)	50.00
TOTAL START-UP COSTS:	**$2650.00**

* Business license - no fee for new business.

Operating expenses would include monthly operating costs and are not included in a start-up cost sheet.

The initial costs will vary, depending on individual circumstances.

PRACTICAL II-1:

Prepare a start-up cost sheet of what you will need to start your business and what the costs (estimated costs okay) will be.

Your Business Entity

In starting out any business, you want to determine what your legal format is going to be for structuring your business. Each has its own uses and limitations.

The business entity format you choose to make depends on your decision of how you want to run your company.

These formats are:

- Sole proprietorship - unincorporated, owned by one person.

- Partnership - unincorporated, two or more persons who profit as co-owners.

- Corporation - a separate legal and tax entity from the owners (a C Corporation, referring to Chapter C of the IRS code).

  → S Corporation (referring to Chapter S of the IRS code). Begins as a C Corporation. (Taxed like a partnership or sole proprietorship rather than as a separate entity).

  → Non-profit corporation - an organization registered with IRS declaring federal and state tax exemption.

- Limited Liability Company (LLC) - not a partnership or a corporation. (Combines advantages of a corporation's limited liability with a partnership's pass-through taxation.)

You'll find pros and cons in each of these formats. Therefore, in deciding how you want to set up your business, you may consider consulting your attorney for advice on what structure best suits your needs.

If you are considering becoming a corporation, (either stock or nonprofit), a limited liability company or a partnership (limited, limited liability, or general), you must file with the Secretary of State's Office.

Setting Up Your Business Operations

A person going into business is now under the title of a "business owner" and will need to take responsibility as one. Some basic business knowledge is necessary to set up your new business.

Fictitious Name Filing (DBA)

A DBA (Doing Business As -- also referred to as Fictitious Name) is a legal procedure business owners are required to do if using a fictitious name. This would not apply to corporations and owners doing business under their own name. On the other hand, if you plan to use your own name as part of the business name, (i.e., Smith & Associates) you must file a Fictitious Business Name statement.

A Fictitious Business Name with "corp." or "Inc." is not allowed unless you want to file a DBA for a corporation with the same name.

For example, "Smith's Organizing Service" would not be required to file a fictitious business name -- however, "Smith and Company" would be required to file a fictitious business name.

A person can file a DBA within 40 days of starting their business, and the filing of a DBA takes an average of 4-7 business days. This is followed with publishing the fictitious business name in a legally adjudicated newspaper (for 4 weeks). You'll need to get proof of publication.

A DBA is necessary in opening a business bank account (unless you are using your own name as part of the business name).

Business License and Permits

Each state has different business licensing requirements. A business license or permit (a business tax certificate) is required for most entities doing business within their city limits. Contact your local city or government offices (usually in the courthouse) for information about licensing requirements in your area. Fees, if any, are small. For new businesses, most cities do not charge a fee.

You'll need to establish the type of business you have (i.e., business services) and file for your license with the City Clerk, Finance Dept -- Tax and Permit Division.

Any businesses selling merchandise must obtain a Seller's Permit with the State Board of Equalization -- Sales / Tax Division.

Employer Identification Number (EIN or SSN)

Employers with employees, business partnerships, and corporations, must obtain an Employer Identification Number from the I.R.S. Otherwise, a business owner may choose to use their Social Security Number (SSN) for IRS identification.

This ID will be used when clients give you a W4 Form and when filing taxes.

Business Insurance

In establishing an organizing business, one should carry General Liability insurance. This covers negligence of yourself and contractors working for you. It doesn't cover injuries (the client should have workers comp which covers injuries on their premises of others doing work for them).

There is professional organizer Liability insurance available with some insurance agencies that cover a single person only (not anyone working for you on a job). This is under business insurance category for professional organizers.

People who work for themselves at home are not obligated to carry insurance.

Bonding

Getting bonded is not a common practice among professional organizers. Small businesses performing contracting services are required to get bonded, however occasionally a client may ask if you are bonded. When this occurs, and the client intends to hire your services, you can seek to get bonded.

A bond (also referred to as a surety bond) is a third-party obligation promising to pay if the vendor does not fulfill their obligations under a contract. A bond is simply, a financial guarantee that the vendor will honor a business contract. It is not an insurance policy (and does not pay for property damage or personal injury resulting from your work).

Generally, bonding companies will only provide bond coverage in an amount that you can cover with existing liquid assets. Bonding for a sole proprietorship is not very cost-effective.

Your local telephone directory will list bonding services (under "surety bonds").

Filing Taxes

As independent contractors, organizers do not have employee withholding. Therefore, estimated tax payments need to be filed and paid quarterly. This is done from their net income. These quarterly tax payments are due on April 15, June 15, September 15, and January 15.

It is advised that you talk to a tax professional regarding your specific circumstances.

Copyrights and Trademarks

A **copyright** protects a "form of expression" such as writings, designs, and works of art. A copyright is automatic in that anything you write, design, or otherwise conceive, is protected by the copyright laws. This protection generally lasts for your lifetime plus 50 years. A copyright may be registered with the Patent & Trademark Office.

A **trademark** is a word or series of words, a design or graphic that relates to your product, service, or company. A trademark must be registered with the Patent and Trademark Office and cost a few hundred dollars.

A **service mark** is the same as a trademark, except that it identifies and distinguishes the source of a service rather than a product.

To learn more, go to the Patent and Trademark website, www.uspto.gov.

Anyone who intends to trademark their company name should perform a search for that name to see if anyone else owns a trademark on it.

Handling Finances

Keeping Records

To avoid business disaster, keep accurate, up-to-date accounting records. Use these records to control and manage your business and help you understand your business.

This helps a business owner:

- Know how the business is doing at all times

- Be able to understand their costs

- Know where their money is going

- See how much cash is on hand in relation to their liabilities, and perceive any cash crunch or creeping inefficiencies

- Improve their business

A good accountant can help you set up your accounting system and Chart of Accounts, if that's needed. If you're not computerized, consider doing so. Finance software automates the task of managing money and enables an individual to run various financial reports in a few "clicks" of the keyboard.

Popular electronic bookkeeping applications include:

Quicken
QuickBooks
PeachTree

Cash Management

Cash flow means the balance or difference between incoming cash (receipts) and outgoing cash (disbursements). It is measured at the end of a particular time period. In checking accounts, the cash flow would be the difference between checks deposited and checks written.

Making calculated estimates of cash flows and disbursements is what cash management is about. It helps you anticipate your future cash needs.

Cash Flow Report
(SAMPLE)

INCOME

Book sales inc.	843.10
Writing inc.	480.00
Service fees	6280.00
Advertising inc.	235.35
Training inc.	925.00

TOTAL INCOME	8,763.45

EXPENSES

Advertising	237.77
Auto	340.58
Computer/Internet	89.90
Bus Gifts	59.36
Labor	1,365.00
Meals & Enter	342.85
Office Supplies	120.81
Phone	68.45
Postage	57.50
Printing	195.93
Rent	1,500.00
P.O. Box	49.50
Research	202.25
Travel	50.00
Wardrobe	176.35

TOTAL EXPENSES	4,856.25

Finance Reports

Every business should run financial reports on a weekly or monthly basis to let them know how their business is doing. These reports include:

- Cash Flow
- Profit & Loss
- Balance Sheet

It is also a good practice to establish a Budget Sheet to budget your expenditures. In budgeting, expense allocations can be designated for marketing and promotional activities, as well as operational expenses.

A savings reserve set-aside is another good business practice. Try to set-aside 5-10% of your income into a reserve account. This is not an "emergency" account, and should not really be spent except for large purchases (like property).

A Financial Plan is a monthly expense allocation report that a person can create for set-aside expenses. In doing this, you allocate all your income (for the week or month) to the set-aside expenses.

Invoicing Client

There are various invoicing methods used by businesses to bill their clients (see sample). They can do this with:

- Manual invoicing
- Accounting software
- Word-processing or spreadsheets

The invoice would include your organizing service and rates, as well as any expenses -- like, client purchases, auto mileage, travel (airfare, hotel, transportation, and parking).

Invoice
(SAMPLE)

Smith's Organizing

Invoice

Bill To:

Client
Address
City, State, Zip

Invoice #:

Invoice Date:

Customer ID:

Date	Description	Quantity	Rate	Total
	Organizing services	10 hrs	$55.00	$550.00

YOUR COMPANY'S
ADDRESS

ESTABLISHING YOUR BUSINESS

Strategic Planning ⇐

A Business Plan

One tool for managing your business is a business plan. Without a plan, no operation will flow smoothly or achieve great success. We need to have a road map and strategy.

Business plans are not just to raise capital, although this is a primary tool in doing so. Instead, a plan is needed for any owner to see where they are, where they are going, how to get there, and what their market and competition is.

An accountant (who is also a business authority) can work with you as a consultant to assist with business plans (which include cash flow projections) and other important decisions about your company. An attorney who specializes in business is another key advisor for a business owner.

Business plans vary from one to another. Some can be quite extensive, some simple. In starting out an organizing business venture, keep it simple to start. You can build on it later, as you should.

Many of the practical assignments in this book will give you a start on creating your plan. You'll see what skills you have that will become your services, who your targeted market will be, and some marketing strategies.

To give yourself a clearly focused strategy, your business plan should include these sections:

- Executive Summary
- About the Company -- Overview, vision, mission statement, objectives, team, management and organization.
- Products and Services - Product catalog, research and development, types of services.
- Operational Plan - Planned operations, production costs, facilities, customer service
- Market Analysis - Market definition, market research, market segment, customer profile, the overall market, competition, business risks.

- Marketing Plan - Distinctive competence (why you are unique), marketing and sales strategy, advertising and promotion, public relations, sales forecast, pricing, business development activities.
- Financial Plan - Assumptions/Projected cash flow, balance sheets.

A plan is worked and reworked. It evolves as your business evolves. Basically, it can be considered a living entity, as it often takes on a life of its own as you grow.

Mission Statement

In the management role, one will search for effective ways to carry out the organization's mission. A clearly defined Mission Statement is an aid that helps a company focus on its mission.

A Mission Statement is a statement about your vocation (occupation). It is the mission of the organization. -- its production of basic products and services.

An example of a mission statement:

"To provide innovative, practical and top-quality services that save time and improve people's lifestyle and the way they manage their work and themselves. We believe our first responsibility is to the customers who use our products and services."

Goals and Objectives

In creating one's "vision," a business owner will need to set business goals and objectives. There can be long-term goals and short-term goals. In either case, a time-limiter should be placed on each goal.

For example, "To be open for business within 3 months."

Goals are an important part of planning. An organizer who runs their business without goals or plans is heading nowhere.

So, make goals and when you achieve those, make new ones.

The Transition from Part-time to Full-time

If a person plans to keep another job while doing their organizing business part-time, they can phase into full-time operations when jobs increase.

When working your business full-time, it is advised to have enough working capital as an insurance against slow periods which affect one's ability to meet expenses.

Another good measure to take is to set aside a certain percentage of your income each week in a "reserves" account. It is best not to dip into this fund but, if the need arises due to a slow work schedule, you'll have some reserves to keep you going.

Writing Programs

In order to carry out a plan, write a checklist of project steps. This format is called a program.

A program is best laid out with scheduled deadlines to complete task steps. Project management programs help project managers develop a timeline for projects, assign people to tasks, and outline all the actions necessary to complete a project from start to finish.

A program may consist of actions to carry out your tactical plan (tasks and resources), your strategic plan (project phases and goal statements), and your operations plan (project tasks).

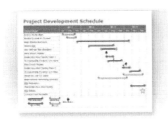

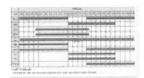

(SAMPLE - Without timelines)

Business Start-up Program

Purpose: To launch my organizing business, and to have people wanting and signing up for my services.

_____ 1.   Implement a work agenda that includes my various hats and routine actions.

_____ 2.   Create an organizing chart of my company's structure.

_____ 3.   Establish accounting method and financial policy. Do set-asides for reserves, promotion, taxes.

_____ 4.   Get business license.

_____ 5.   Get DBA.

_____ 6.   Open business checking account.

_____ 7.   Get business phone line - ensure listed in an "Organizing Services" category.

_____ 8.   Join NAPO and get on a committee.

_____ 9.   Start a Business Plan that includes your services and fees, as well as a Marketing Plan for the first quarter through the fourth quarter.

_____ 10. Create and send out promo postcards to local business mailing list.

_____ 11. Write and send press releases about newsworthy events on a regular basis.

_____ 12. Create work logs and contract form for running business operations.

_____ 13. Create a monthly E-Zine (or newsletter) and send to friends and associates (to start, until a contact database is built up).

_____ 14. Build a media database to submit articles and press releases to.

_____ 15. Research and submit for speaker opportunities.

_____ 16. Get business insurance.

Organization Structure

Any business, no matter how small or how big, needs structure. Activities need to be compartmentalized and flow lines need to be established.

The main reason a business owner should create an organization chart, even if they perform many or all of the duties, is to:

- Establish the flow lines of the various areas
- See how things inter-relate and exchange with each other
- Know what "hats" they need to perform

An organization chart is a blueprint for the company's organizational development. It should be clearly identified in the early stages of planning and implementation of a business venture.

This chart also helps depict the company's needs and those that will become important as the business evolves, as well as the kinds of individuals required to address such responsibilities and hats (see example below).

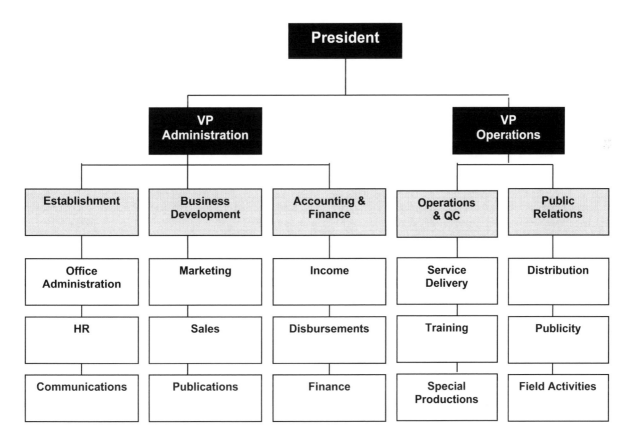

PRACTICAL II-2:

1. Take a look at what divisions and departments your company should have. Create an organization chart for how you want to structure your company.

2. Write your mission statement.

3. Write down your company goals and objectives for the first year in business.

Setting Fees

One of the questions most often asked in regard to running an organizing business are about fee setting.

Today, organizing consultants charge an average of $50.00 per hour for residential and personal organizing and, for business organizing, $75.00 to $150.00 or more per hour.

This kind of standard sets an industry value on organizing services, and is varied based on an individual's notoriety or years of experience.

There are corporations that will pay outside consultants anywhere from $1,000/day to $2,000/day, depending on the project and service.

Professional organizers, who become leaders in their field and author books, do public speaking, and/or deliver seminars and workshops may charge more for their services than other organizers, for instance.

This can act as an incentive for people in this business to expand their income-making endeavors and put their "eggs in different baskets," as the phrase goes.

It is advised that organizers do not offer "Introductory rates" because, most often, they will do the work that is done at regular rates during the introductory service anyway. This also sets a custom that is not easy to break away from which can lock a person into a practice that is being under-charged. The thing to look at is how we value our time.

An organizer can offer special discounts or a free initial consultation (typically a half-hour consultation or diagnostics at start of service that assesses the job project).

If a potential client wishes to meet with the organizer and take a look at the home or business before committing to hire your services, a 1-2 hour minimum should be charged for your visit and consultation.

Fee Structure

Rates can be structured hourly, per diem (daily), weekly, monthly, or by project, depending on the assignment. It is best to get a retainer for monthly service, followed with weekly payments.

Most projects, however, can be offered with sliding scale rates in blocks of hours. One could consider a sliding scale discount for blocks of 10, 15, 20+ hours.

If a client wishes to purchase a block of hours, they would be "locked in" at those rates, even if they buy additional hours to finish up the project.

A client purchasing blocks of hours shows a commitment for the project, and the organizer can typically complete a project without concern the client won't back out after a few hours (leaving an incomplete project).

If hourly rates are $85.00 per hour, a sliding scale might be offered as:

$750.00 for 10 hours @ $75/hr
$1050.00 for 15 hours @ $70/hr
$1300.00 for 20 hours @ $65/hr

These packages are purchased at start of service, in advance.

Calculating Fees

There are some simple factors to keep in mind when setting your fees. They are:

- Your desired annual income.
- The total number of hours you want to work weekly (hours with client, hours with business admin and marketing).
- The number of client hours you plan to work each week (hours with client only).

To calculate your fee structure, let's break it down into a formula:

1. Multiply the client hours by the weekly hours you plan to work (deducting for vacation, sick leave, holidays) - gives <u>you total annual hours</u>.

2. Divide the annual hours by your **desired** annual income - and this gives you the <u>hourly rate</u> you should charge.

EXAMPLE:

$50,000 - Annual income desired
40 hrs - Weekly hours (20 client hrs.)

20 (billable hrs.) X 45 wks. (with vacation, sick days, holidays) = 900 hrs./yr.

900 / 50,000 = $55/hr.

Setting fees and structuring your rates will change as you grow and become more experienced (to charge higher rates). Start off with a rate you are comfortable with, but not below industry standards -- it makes the profession look bad!

Business Organization Tools

Even though the organizing business requires some of the same business tools as any business, it may also warrant a more customized approach in determining the type of materials which will work best (most fitted for an organizer's needs). Below you'll find some "Tools of the Trade" recommendations.

Business Materials

Organizer/planner. Because an organizer often spends time "out in the field" (on location at a job), it is best to have an organizing planner which acts as their "field office." This, of course, would be customized for the individual's needs, yet, at the same time, should feature these basic parts:

- Calendar
- Appointment scheduler (daily or weekly)
- Task lists (daily and master lists)
- Contacts (phone number/addresses)

Other sections can be categorized for projects, notes, logs, reference, information, ideas, personal, etc. -- whatever is suited for one's own use.

Being in the organizing business, we need to be a role model and set a precedence in how we manage our affairs. By keeping our planning information in one place, for example, may inspire or prompt an observer to do the same.

Info Packet. It is important and desirable to keep information packages ready to send out which contain:

- Company brochure (or fact sheet of services)
- Profile or biography (of Organizer)
- Photo
- Client reference list
- Client testimonials

To be included, when available:
- Press clippings
- Published articles
- Company newsletter (or promotional flyer)

Thomas Guide / maps. Organizers who perform work in the field (on a job site), should have city maps, preferably a Thomas Guide, to establish the best route on getting someplace. In most cases the client will provide directions, however, it is recommended that one also look at a map to get a better view of where they're going.

Portfolio. Keeping an album collection of your work is a good promotional tool, as well as a nice running record of your achievements. It can contain items such as client testimonial letters, your published articles, press, photographs of work projects, and any examples of your work, as accumulated.

Office Supplies

Invoice or sales receipts. Each business has its own methods of operation, including its billing system. Contractors in the field sometimes prefer to carry a sales receipt book, or invoice book, to write a receipt for money paid on site. Some prefer to prepare an invoice in advance by computer. In either case, get pre-payment for your service.

Business cards and stationary. When setting up a business, business cards are a vital tool in making a statement about your company, in addition to being used as a promotional tool.

Letterhead and envelopes are standard business materials. To add a graphics appeal, consider having a logo designed for your company.

Files and binders. Depending on an individual's preference, information on a subject can be stored and categorized in notebook binders or files.

Some people may find it easier to organize their marketing and promotional material in a binder, for instance. Another subject category to consider storing in sections within a binder, if desired, are media contacts and special projects.

No matter what information and filing system is chosen to fit an operation, it should be suited to an individual's preference.

Misc. materials. This would include any other office supplies which assist in the flow of operations, such as baskets for mail and communications, organizing shelves for paper material, desktop files for action or project folders, bookshelves for trade and reference books, and any other organizing items needed for business flow.

Field Equipment

Label maker *(optional)*. Supply manufacturers, such as Brother, have made a convenient tool which enables an Organizer to generate nice looking, professional labels on the spot.

Tape recorder *(optional)*. Although having a tape recorder is not an essential business tool, it does allow an Organizer (who spends a great deal of time out in the field) to note their thoughts and ideas while on the road. This is much easier than trying to write something down while driving.

Another benefit of a tape recorder is recording a list of actions to do following a meeting.

Office Equipment

Communications equipment. This would include your phone system (one or two lines, etc.), preferably a business line with answering machine or voice mail to retrieve messages, and any other means in which to enable a person to communicate easily and swiftly.

Depending on a person's operations, cellular phones and pagers are effective methods to ensure swift communications when they are out in the field a lot.

Other communications equipment to assist with business operations would include a fax and a computer modem, however these are not mandatory tools to run this type of business.

Computer equipment (optional). In this day and age it is best to be computerized with a computer system to meet one's needs. A person can, however, run a business without being computerized.

Either way, office equipment is needed to handle various business tasks such as: Financial record-keeping, Word-processing, Spreadsheets, Contact management.

Copy machine (optional). This is a costly investment, yet, in the long run, will provide better time efficiency; for a home business owner.

PRACTICAL II-3:

1) List the business tools and office equipment you have

2) List the business tools and office equipment you will need.

Setting Up Your Home Office

There are many benefits to working from home. There are also some pitfalls to working at home, if certain policies are not enforced on oneself.

One of the pitfalls is home interruptions. Without proper discipline, an individual can lose valuable time in growing their business if they allow constant, personal interference during their working hours.

This is not to say you should not speak to anyone in your family during work hours, this is only to suggest that one make certain rules that everyone in the family should try to honor and respect.

Home Office Space

Having a room in your home for your office space is important, even if it's a section of a den that has clearly defined parameters. A desk, a file cabinet, and a bookshelf would be among the kind of office furniture recommended to set up your home office space.

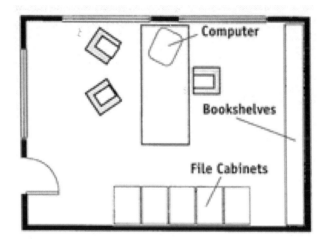

Working Hours and Routine

Setting your work hours and a routine are key factors to achieving the kind of control a business person needs. Anyone consulting time management knows this. Establish a work routine and make a commitment to follow it as closely as possible. Certain days of the week should also be allocated to business development and marketing activities.

Work Agenda - SAMPLE

	Morning 7:30-9:30 a.m.	Late A.M. 10 - noon	Afternoon 1 - 6:00 p.m.	Evening 7- 10:00 p.m.
MON	*Workout* Admin & calls	Finance/bill paying	Jobs/Projects Marketing	*Off*
TUES	Admin & calls	Jobs/Projects	Jobs/Projects	*Off*
WED	*Workout* Admin & calls	Jobs/Projects	Jobs/Projects Marketing	*Off*
THUR	Admin & calls Web updates	Jobs/Projects	Jobs/Projects	*Off*
FRI	*Workout* Admin & calls	Jobs/Projects	Jobs/Projects Statistics Weekly plan	*Off*
SAT	*Off*	*Off*	*Off*	*Off*
SUN	*Workout*	*Off*	*Off*	*Off*

PRACTICAL II-4:

1. Observe what work habits and routines others have to improve your operations and delivery. Make a note of these.

2. Establish a work routine in which you and your home business can operate within (and includes time for marketing actions, appointments, special projects, administration, and planning.

RUNNING YOUR BUSINESS

Project Preliminaries

Terms of a Work Project

Every job should be confirmed and documented with a "Job Order" or "Letter of Agreement." (See samples at the end of this chapter). Whatever you call it, this sets the rates and terms of the project.

Part of the terms should include a cancellation clause. This sets a standard which will help an organizer control their weekly income expectancy.

If you expect income on a given day that week and the job is postponed or cancelled at the last minute, this can create a problem. Therefore, it is good policy to charge 50 % of the agreed upon fee if the scheduled date is cancelled less than 48 hours.

With some regular clients, diplomacy is needed to maintain good relations, but be careful to waive this policy more than once.

Hiring Assistants

If a project warrants the need for another (or other) organizers, a sub-contractor agreement should be signed. The reason for an agreement is to substantiate the terms of the relationship and, most importantly, to secure client ownership.

A Subcontractor will require a 1099 at tax time, if exceeds $600.00. Be sure to get their social security number at the time of hiring their services.

Qualifying a Client

Going out on a meeting should result in a work project. Usually, this can be guaranteed by qualifying the potential client over the phone.

By discussing the service you will provide and your rates on the phone, you will, most likely, be able to determine if your service and fees are acceptable to the prospective client.

Once established, you can schedule a consultation meeting (or a half-hour free consultation can be offered at the start of service). Some organizers schedule this first meeting on the same day the job is scheduled to be carried out (if closed over the phone), others schedule the job at the meeting for a later date.

Cost Estimates

Try to avoid providing cost estimates for organizing projects, as it is very difficult to determine the length of time on most projects. Corporations, on the other hand, may require a quote and proposal. In this case, careful calculations need to be determined for providing accurate cost quotes on the project.

In responding to a request for a cost estimate, let the person know that, in this line of work, it is tricky to provide such a quote. One drawer can open up a lengthy task or it can work out to be a quick task.

You can find out what areas the person wants to organize and get their description of what they feel the problem is. This can give you an idea of what's involved.

The variables of a work project are:

- the client
- the amount of things to sort through
- added tasks not covered in the assessment

An organizer can give a rough cost quote to someone over the phone without being there and seeing the problem. For example, in dealing with a 2,000 square foot home, it can be estimated that the project might take approximately 5-10 hours per room. A very cluttered garage, for instance, may take more time.

One approach to avoid giving time estimates is to sell an organizing project in blocks of hours (10, 15, 20, etc) and, inform them that the project will "take as long as it takes." You'll want to get payment for a block of hours up front at the start of the project, which indicates that the person is committed to completing the project.

Job Project Analysis

It may be helpful to have a questionnaire form with questions to ask at the first meeting which will give you a clear overview of the problems and priorities the client has. This information helps establish what needs to be done, what priorities will be taken, and should even help to determine which systems to implement before starting the project.

It might be a good idea to have some catalogs that show organizing products you'd like to recommend, or just to spark ideas for solutions on creating an organized environment.

Before the organizing project is started, it is best that the client purchases the recommended products or tools. It may just be that maybe they just need to have some boxes on hand before you begin.

A Needs Assessment

A "Needs Assessment" is a service that is charged to the client as a paid consultation (the term I used to refer to this action as was a "Diagnostic Survey" before NAPO coined an industry term for it).

This is to assess (evaluate) what the project will entail for the client. In this survey, the organizer assesses the area and notes the problem spots.

From this, the organizer can recommend organizing solutions and suggest certain purchases that aid in doing the organizing project.

Why Conduct A Needs Assessment?

A Needs Assessment is done to learn and discover.

- Learn what problems exist
- Discover what causes the problems

The client doesn't always know what the problem is. They just see the mess, and they think the problem is the mess. The mess, however, is just a symptom of the problem.

To diagnose problems and problem areas, you'll do this by:

- Fact-finding from a client interview or questionnaire
- Observations from a walk-through

When Do You An Assessment?

The value of an assessment derives from knowing what is needed and wanted from a client and for a project. Depending on circumstances, it can be carried out either:

- at the beginning of the organizing project, same day
- at the initial consultation, first appointment
- when giving estimates, first appointment

Assessment Objectives

The goals of the assessment for the professional organizer are:

- to gather information
- to clarify job perimeters
- to define problem areas
- to find cause of problem areas
- to determine needs
- to create a strategy for project

The objectives for client align with these goals.

- to find out the real problem
- to understand the problem
- to fix the problem

Assessment Format

The 5 steps and sequence of actions in doing an assessment are:

1) Gather information with client survey questionnaire
2) Diagnose area with a thorough walk-through
3) Make evaluations of problems and problem areas
4) Provide recommendations / solutions to handle the problems
5) Write up a project plan

Making Observations

To observe means to:

- become aware of, especially through careful and directed attention.
- make a systematic or scientific observation.
- look and listen.

Observation is <u>NOT</u>:

- asking someone a question
- making guesses or assumptions
- imagining something is there
- believing something to be there

There is a difference between speculation and what is actually there.

For example, a cluttered purse is an incorrect observation. It's a label. What do you actually see? You'll notice that what you actually see is a purse with many things sticking out of it. Get what I mean?

The Discovery Process

To discover what problems exist, one must gather information. You'll get facts from the client with survey questionnaire or interview questions.   You'll see what's there with a walk-through. Don't be afraid to get permission from client to open drawers, closets, cabinets, cupboards.

Look and see what's around. Notice if there are:

- Cluttered and messy areas
- Piles of homeless items
- Paper clutter
- Unnecessary furniture, or too much furniture in space
- Furniture surfaces that unnecessary items on them
- Things on floor
- Storage and space issues
- Items that do not have an organizing tool to be stored in
- Collectibles that are scattered around the area and not displayed well
- Photographs that are stored in various places
- Items that are placed inconveniently and not easily accessible
- Items that are not used often out in living spaces, not in storage areas
- Loose items of like-categories not grouped together and contained
- Traffic areas that are blocked or hindered with items around it

---

Be like Sherlock Holmes -- find out who, what, when, where, and why.

- Who uses the space? Who needs to use the space?
- What is that space intended for? What is its function?
- What do they want to do in that space?
- What are their habits and routines?
- What furniture or equipment is unnecessary in that space?
- What does the space look like, and how does it make you feel?
- What kind of storage solutions are there?
- When is the space most used, and by whom?
- Where are items supposed to be that are somewhere else?
- Where do they perform paper and work-related tasks?
- Where are they supposed to perform paper and work-related tasks?
- Why isn't the space being used the way it is supposed to?

These type of questions (and more) are part of the fact-finding and observation process. The answers to these questions should provide the whole story, and give the underlying reason for the problem areas -- the basic reason.

- Visible problems made from observations show the *symptom* of the problem.
- Questions about the observations give the real reason, the *real problem*.

The Evaluation

After making observations and gathering facts from client, one can now evaluate the problem(s) and make a problem statement.

Observation: Jammed file cabinets
Facts: difficulty storing and retrieving files - using the Alpha system.
Problem: files not being archived, not enough file cabinets for amount of active files, no effective filing system.

Observation: Papers in piles and loose on top desk surface.
Facts: can't find needed paper.
Problem: no paper flow system.

Observation: Clothes closet overflowing with items stored inside that don't belong there, no order for hanging clothes.
Facts: unable to find and retrieve clothes easily.
Problem: No storage systems for closet, too many clothes for the space.

Observation: Garage overflowing with boxes and loose, open items.
Facts: unable to use garage for cars, can't find anything in garage.
Problem: No storage system for garage.

Recommendations

After an evaluation, offer solutions. In the case of the jammed files:

Solution: Purchase another 4-drawer file cabinet, sort files and archive old files, create new filing system using Subject classifications.

You'll want to keep in mind and determine:

- Priorities of tasks
- Organizing products needed
- Furniture needed / not needed
- Space solutions
- Storage systems
- Functionality
- Paper flow
- Aesthetics

Product Solutions

- Browse through catalogs
- Internet shopping
- Show product portfolio

Suggested catalogs include:

Office supply catalogs	Harriet Carter
Lillian Vernon	Ikea
Specialty stores	Gift catalogs

Internet shopping:

The Container Store	TheStorageStore.com
StacksandStacks.com	GetOrgInc.com
HomeOrganization.com	Organize-it.com
OrganizeEverything.com	SpaceSavers.com
OrganizedHome.com	StorageWorks.com

Writing The Plan

Create a Project Plan using your observations, evaluations, and recommendations. The solutions should include recommended purchases to make. The organizer provides a copy of the Project Plan to client (use carbon).

- Recommendations
- Solutions
- Purchases to make
- Project tools
- Project sheet

Taking The Next Step

The final product of the assessment is client understands what's needed and wants to start project.

- Client sees big picture.
- Client knows what needs to be done.
- Client understands what's needed to carry out project.
- Client agrees to Project Plan.
- Client wants to get started on project.

A Needs Assessment Form (for a home)
(SAMPLE ONLY)

LOCATION: (Common areas) LIVING ROOM, FAMILY ROOM		
		Observations & Fact-finding
1)		What types of clutter are noticeable around area?
2)		Are there items on the floor other than furniture and décor items?
3)		Are there piles of paper in area? How many? Where?
4)		How does the room make you feel? How does it make the client feel?
5)		Is there unnecessary furniture in room that doesn't serve a needed function?
6)		Is there too much furniture for the size of the room?
7)		Are there collectibles in the area? Are they displayed well, or scattered in various places in room?
8)		Are traffic areas blocked? What is blocking them?
9)		Is the space plan for the room set up efficiently? What isn't efficient about it?
10)		What kind of activities takes place in this area? Are any of these activities designated to be performed elsewhere?
11)		Are there items in the room that are not needed?
12)		What does the client want to do in this area that they are unable to do?
13)		What are the client's goals and objectives for this room?
LOCATION: HOME OFFICE AREA (include the above with these additions):		
14)		Is the office equipment and furniture set up efficiently?
15)		Are filing cabinets jammed?
16)		Can the client find files easily?
17)		Are papers lying around the desk and other surfaces?
18)		Are there organizing tools for the desktop? (file baskets, file holders, etc.)
19)		Are there shelves for books and materials?
20)		Are there any storage issues?

		LOCATION: KITCHEN, DINING ROOM, AND BATHROOM AREAS
21)		What type of clutter is in the area?
22)		Are the cabinets / cupboards cluttered or jammed?
23)		Is the space set up efficiently?
24)		Are there storage issues? What kind?
25)		Are like-items grouped together and/or contained in storage containers?
26)		Besides clutter, what do you notice about this area that is not ideal?
27)		What does the client want to do in this area that they are unable to do?
28)		What are the client's goals and objectives for this area?
		LOCATION: BEDROOM AND CLOSET AREAS
29)		What type of clutter is in the area?
30)		Is the space set up efficiently?
31)		Besides clutter, what do you notice about this area that is not ideal?
32)		Are clothes closets jammed? Are items on the floor that doesn't belong there?
33)		Are shoes and accessories stored neatly?
34)		Are dresser drawers neat or messy?
35)		What does the client want to achieve in this area that they have been unable to achieve?
36)		What are the client's goals and objectives for this area?
		LOCATION: GARAGE AND STORAGE AREAS
37)		What type of clutter is visible in the area?
38)		How many boxes are stored in this area?
39)		Does client know what is in the boxes stored?
40)		Are there small loose items on the shelves or around the area that are not contained in storage bins / containers? What kind of items?
41)		Is furniture or items stored in the area that the client doesn't want displayed or placed in the home? What is the value of these items to the client (not monetary)?
42)		What are the client's goals and objectives for this area?

PRACTICAL III-1:

1) Make observations of a room and note down what you observed.
2) Perform a Needs Assessment with the form example in this book.
3) Write down your recommendations with solutions to the problem(s).

The Need for Proposals

Occasionally, for corporate jobs or large projects, an organization will request a proposal. This task is sometimes done after a preliminary meeting, or before a meeting even takes place (i.e., bid requests).

A lot of time can go into these proposals and, unfortunately we cannot bill the potential client for our time spent preparing it. Nor can we charge for most initial meeting presentations. However, a well-written proposal can often lead to a very lucrative project.

Depending on the project, there are steps that will be required in order to develop the proposal. These can include (or not) the following:

- Meeting with management executives

- Information gathering (Needs Assessment)

- Formulate interview questions for initial research on the problems

- Compile a summary and determine client priorities, issues, cause of problems

- Write proposal

Variables in the Process

From the initial contact to the "close of sale," each project will vary in the process. A typical flow chart is a simple one:

- Potential client calls, discuss needs on phone, schedule job appointment (closing the sale).

- Prepare Job Order (or Letter of Agreement contract).

- Arrive on scheduled day and begin with a preliminary assessment of the problem areas. Make any necessary recommendations and purchase requests.

- Collect payment for project, if working on retainer of services.

- Start job project.

More steps can be entered into this process, depending on the needs and/or requests of the potential client, and the size or scope of the project.

These steps can be amended to suit particular circumstances.

For example:

- Potential client calls, discuss needs on phone, schedule an initial meeting.
- Attend meeting, possibly give a presentation (for corporate clients).
- Assess problems and recommend solution and priorities.
- Get hired for the job. Collect deposit for services.
- If no proposal necessary, create Job Order or Letter of Agreement contract and get payment.
- Schedule start of project date.
- Start job project.

Writing Proposals

In writing a proposal, there are various elements that should be included in it. This book is not intended to teach you how to write one, however here are some things to include when putting one together:

- Summary
- Research methodology and results
- Recommendations (your plan - proposed solution)
- Scope of work (your approach)
- Project Costs and schedule
- Company background information
- Addendums

Company Overview
   Management Profile

Our Understanding
   Primary Objectives
   Secondary Objectives

The Plan
   Proposed Solution

Our Approach
   Scope of Work

Project Costs & Schedule
   Project Schedule
   Professional Fees & Costs

A project schedule for a filing system may look like this:

	Days						
	1	2	3	4	5	6	7
Information gathering	X						
Draft classifications		X					
Data inventory (folders)			X	X			
Data entry					X	X	
Review and finalize							X

For a home project, it may look like this:

Task	Day 1	Day 2	Day 3	Day 4
Master BR				
Master closets				
Office area				(papers)
Family Rm				

Task	Day 5	Day 6	Day 7	Day 8
Guest Rm				
Spare Rm				
Laundry Rm				
Kitchen				
Living Rm				

Task	Day 9	Day 10	Day 11	Day 12
Art-craft Rm				
Closets				
Hall cabinets				
Garage				(sorting)

Task	Day 13	Day 14		
Garage sale	(pricing, preps - for garage sale)	(organization)		

Project Estimates

Some potential clients may request an estimate and/or to meet with you prior to hiring your services. Because of the nature of our kind of work, estimating how long an organizing project will take is almost impossible, depending on the job project, of course.

However, some projects can be estimated. Closet designers, for instance, can often calculate the time and cost on organizing closets.

Organizing clutter, on the other hand, is one which you never know what you're getting into until you get into it. The length of time on such a project has too many variables, such as:

- How fast or slow the client is you are working with in making decisions on what to let go or keep.

- Additional boxes or areas not otherwise seen visibly from your initial assessment.

- Added work based on what is uncovered during the organizing project.

An organizer can avoid giving estimates on time by informing the potential client about the above variables. Most all potential clients will understand and be okay with this.

That is why it is a good idea to offer sliding-scale rates on organizing projects and perform the task in stages. Based on their organization needs and the size of the project, an organizer can safely make a judgment whether the client should start off with 10 hours, 15 hours, or 20 hours. Inform them that they will be "locked in" at those rates and can purchase additional hours, as necessary, to complete the project.

Lack of Qualifications or Resources

At any time that you receive a call or make contact with a potential client that involves doing a project you don't feel qualified to do or don't have time to do, you can either:

- Refer the job to another organizer
- Sub-contract the job to another organizer

Ideally, you should find an organizer who can do the job and hire them as a sub-contractor under your organization. Charge the client your normal rates and hire the organizer at 40% of that rate (you take 60%). As the contractor, you'll be responsible for the overall supervision of the project, the administration, collecting monies, and distributing payment to the organizer.

If you decide to refer the job to someone else, let the potential client know you will refer another organizer for the job. In referring the job elsewhere, ask the organizer if they offer a referral commission and what it is. If they don't, find someone who does. Don't just give away business -- that's bad business.

Client Administration

Billing Clients

As mentioned in setting rates, full payment of fees should be collected at the start of the project. This avoids an organizer having to try and collect money later, after delivery of services.

This can't always be the case with some business clients or corporate projects. If payment terms are arranged for monthly, bi-monthly, or weekly billing (of hours delivered), be sure to collect a deposit up front as a retainer for your services.

Client Files

Setting up and maintaining good files are important in running any business. A typical client file would consist of:

- Job Order agreement
- Client invoices
- Contact Sheet
- Job assessment and/or project checklist
- Needs Assessment (if performed)
- Client correspondence
- Work hour logs

It is a good idea for big projects to also keep a client project file. This file would contain all work-related papers concerning the project.

Client Testimonials

When a work project is complete, it is a good time to get the satisfied client to write a testimonial or letter of recommendation.

A service questionnaire can be filled out by the client that includes a section to prompt them to write about their achievements as a result of your service.

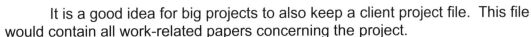

Client Follow-Up

It is also good business to schedule a follow-up call or follow-up maintenance with the client so they know you care about how they are doing down the road. When building up regular business, some clients will be on-going and require routine maintenance, especially if they do not have a secretary or assistant to help them stay organized or manage affairs on their own.

By staying in touch with clients, an organizer may often find other projects to do for them, and visa-versa.

Work Records and Logs

Admin Records

Keeping good work records is an important administrative function of a business owner. For an Organizer, I recommend the following records:

- Client (or Job Order) Log
- Hours Log
- Telephone message Log
- Mileage Log
- Statistical graphs

Job Log

A good way to get an overview of jobs is to maintain a log which provides: Date of Job Order (or Agreement), client name, description of job, referred by source, and fee. This information can be helpful in many ways, especially if you want to refer to something quickly or tally up source data.

Hours Log

A log to track hours on a job project may or may not be necessary, depending on the Organizer's work. If, however, an Organizer sells a block of hours and delivers them over a two to three day, or weekly schedule, this log helps keep record of hours bought and used.

Phone Log

Phone messages can be recorded on either a duplicate message pad, a spiral notebook, or a pre-printed voice-mail log book. To track advertising or promotional endeavors, one can also note the source of the caller (i.e., Daily News or flyer).

Mileage Log

For tax purposes, the mileage log is very important. As a business owner, mileage is tax deductible and needs to be recorded for proper documentation.

Statistical Graphs

Statistic graphs are helpful in getting an overview of how you are doing. When you keep weekly income graphs, for example, you can see your company's progress.

By measuring income, promotion sent out, new business, billable hours, hours delivered, and anything that helps one look at their progress (or lack of progress) is an essential tool for any business owner.

These graphs give a prospective of all the activities in the company. By being able to see what is going on in their company, proper strategies and plans can be implemented to straighten out a failing area or improve a growing area.

If I'm not 'playing a game' with myself, I might impede my company's growth potential. In a group, certain game plans can pull everyone together as a team. For a one-person operation, an individual can operate at a higher level by applying the same principle.

It's one thing to keep logs on production activities, and it's another to graph them. When you can actually SEE dollars or numbers measured on a graph, it allows a person to step in fast and plan for the next strategic move in the battle, if you view yourself on the battlefield of business.

PRACTICAL III-2:

Determine an overall master list of what you will need to do to get started in your organizing business.

Attachments of Sample Forms

Use the sample forms provided
to get an idea of the
information you can use on
your own business forms.

Please respect and honor
these as you would like others
to respect and honor
your rights and work.

These forms are not to be used
for personal financial gain by developing,
or assisting in the development of,
materials for your own or another's benefit.

Thank you.

SAMPLE

JOB ORDER

Client	_____	**Date:**	_____
Contact Person:	_____	**Title:**	_____
Phone #	_____	**Fax #:**	_____
Address:	_____	**Ref. by:**	_____
City/State/Zip:	_____	**Rate: $**	_____

Job Description: Residential organizing services: (detailed description here, as desired).

In consideration for the furnishing of services by (YOUR COMPANY), Client and (YOUR COMPANY) hereby acknowledge, understand and agree to the following:

Payment: Full payment of is due and payable upon start of service for blocks of hours, with hourly fees due and payable upon delivery of service. Non-refundable.

Delivery: Production and delivery schedules shall be set by mutual agreement between Client and (YOUR COMPANY). All creative Work to have final approval by Client.

Cancellation Fee: Cancellation of ·a scheduled appointment must be done within 48 hours prior to the date scheduled. Cancellation of a scheduled date with less than 48 hem notice will be billed at 50% of the agreed upon rate and will be payable immediately.

Performance Guarantee: If the Client is not satisfied with the performance or product of work upon reasonable cause, (YOUR COMPANY) agrees to provide one hour of service at no additional charge to Client. Any claims for dissatisfaction of service must be made in writing by the Client within (7) seven days of delivery of any part of the work. Failure to make claim within this period is final acceptance of work in complete fulfillment of this Job Order.

Miscellany: Upon Client's authorization to commence work, the terms of this Job Order shall be binding upon the parties. This Job Order constitutes the entire understanding between the parties; its terms can be modified only by a written amendment to this Job Order, signed by both parties.

Agreement of the Job Order makes this form into a binding contract subject to the terms and conditions on this form. _Please sign and return original Order to (YOUR COMPANY). Keep a copy for your own records._

CONTRACTOR:	_____	**CLIENT:**	_____
Signature:	_____	**Signature:**	_____
Date:	_____	**Date:**	_____

SAMPLE

LETTER OF AGREEMENT

Dear

This letter will serve to confirm the details and arrangements of our agreement, per our discussion. As a full service organizing company I will provide the following office systems, based on your needs:

1) REORGANIZE EXISTING FILING SYSTEM

    a) Establish customized subject categories based on your company's operations.

    b) Arrange file drawers with workable, easy to retrieve groups of labeled folders, all relating to subject category headings.

    c) Set up a Master Index for subject files to list where to file or retrieve papers.

2) ORGANIZE INFORMATION SYSTEMS

    a) Review existing methods on retrieving Information (aside from file system) and, as needed, provide methods to find Information fast and easy.

    b) Set up any methods which increase efficiency for distributing company information (such as information packs, standard form letters, etc.).

    c) Implement use of particular office products which help organize special items (such as magazines, business came, etc.).

    d) *(Optional)* Institute any tracking systems needed to assist with production or project activities (including contact management, if necessary).

3) ORGANIZE PAPERS

    a) Sort any piles of paper which don't have "a home" or not filed away and set up necessary folders for these documents.

    b) Provide method to manage paper and establish any systems which help handle paper flow (baskets, desktop file holder, organizing shelves, etc.).

The fee for organizing office systems is $_____ for a five hour block or $_____ hourly, payable upon delivery of service. Any materials needed to implement particular systems are at the expense of the client, upon authorization.

Looking forward to a new business relationship with you.

Sincerely,

(your signature)

                              _____   _____

                                  Client signature   Date

SUB-CONTRACTOR'S AGREEMENT

AGREEMENT made as of _____, 20__, between **YOUR COMPANY** (hereinafter referred to as "The Company"), and _____ (Hereinafter referred to as "Sub-Contractor").

WHEREAS, The Company operates a professional organizing service; in consideration of the foregoing premises and the mutual covenants hereinafter set forth and other valuable considerations, the parties hereto agree as follows:

1. **Duties of the Parties**. This agreement shall provide the terms under which the Sub-contractor and The Company shall henceforth do business.

a) The Company shall be solely responsible for soliciting work, negotiating and processing job orders, maintaining and collecting accounts receivable, and the disbursements of Sub-Contractor's pay.
b) Sub-contractor shall perform and be solely responsible for carrying out assigned and scheduled Job Orders in a timely manner.

2. **Relationship of the Parties**. The parties hereto are independent entities and nothing contained in this Agreement shall be construed to constitute the Sub-contractor an employee, partner, joint venture, or any similar relationship with or of The Company. Further, the Sub-contractor hereby indemnifies The Company against any claim by the Sub-contractor with respect to injuries or damages sustained while working on a The Company assignment or caused while traveling.

3. **Assignment**. This Agreement shall not be assignable to another sub-contractor by Sub-contractor.

4. **Confidentiality**. Sub-Contractor shall hold in confidence all materials belonging to The Company or its clients.

5. **Ownership**. Any work created by Sub-contractor for a client of The Company shall be the property of The Company's client. Sub-contractor agrees not to solicit or conduct business with any clients of The Company for his/her own personal or business endeavors during employment and/or for a period of (3) three years after termination of this Agreement.

6. **Termination**. Either party may terminate this Agreement at any time without written notice.

7. **Payment**. Sub-contractor shall submit hours of service delivered each week by Friday at 6:00 PM and provide a written invoice to The Company. Payment will be made within two to three working days.

8. **Penalties**. In the event the Sub-contractor is in default of any of its obligations with a client of The Company or delivers unsatisfactory service with a client of The Company, there will be a penalty to include a deduction of service hours performed by Sub-contractor.

9. **Expenses**. The Company agrees to reimburse the Sub-contractor for authorized expenses incurred with assignment, provided that such expenses shall be approved beforehand by The Company or client of The Company and supported by receipts.

10. **Term**. This Agreement shall have a term of one year, after which it is automatically renewed annually for periods of one year.

11. **Miscellany**. This Agreement contains the entire understanding between the parties and may not be modified, amended, or changed except by an instrument in writing signed by both parties. This Agreement shall be binding upon the parties hereto.

WHEREOF, the parties have signed this Agreement as of the date first set forth above.

_____   _____
YOUR COMPANY Authorized Representative   Sub-Contractor Name

_____   _____
Signature   Signature

BUSINESS CONSULTATION QUESTIONNAIRE

Company: _____   Date: _____

Contact: _____   Title: _____

Phone: _____   Fax: _____

Product/Service: _____   # Employees: _____

1. What would you like us to do for you and your company?

2. What kind of problems do you encounter with your work?

3. What are you interested in handling the most?

4. How do you envision the way your company should be?

5. Are you overwhelmed with managing your paper flow?

6. Do you feel you have a workable filing system in your area? Your company?

7. What area(s) of your company would you say appear overloaded?

8. What area is most backed-up with incomplete actions / projects?

9. Are there policies and guidelines for the company and its operations?

10. Are there job descriptions for every job/position with documentation manuals? If not, which positions do not have this?

11. What would you like us to help you achieve the most?

JOB ORDER / NEW CLIENT LOG

Date	Client	Description	Source	Fee
	Jane Doe	Home organizing	YP	$55/hr
	Jones Construction	Filing system	Ref.	$75/hr

Project Log

Client: Jones Construction   Project: Organize 3 offices

Date	Hours	Description
1-12-01	5	Sorted/organized clutter and paper piles / Jean's office
1-13-01	5	Sorted/organized paper / Ron's office
1-13-01	5	Sorted/organized paper / Bill's office
1-14-01	5	Reorganized main central files
		Project complete: 20 hrs.

PROMO OUT LOG

Date Sent	Mailing list	Main doc	Inserts	Quantity
	Glendale Chamber	Postcard - tips		210
	Burbank Chamber	Postcard - tips		155
	Studio City Chamber	Intro letter	Spring special flyer	134

STATISTICAL GRAPH

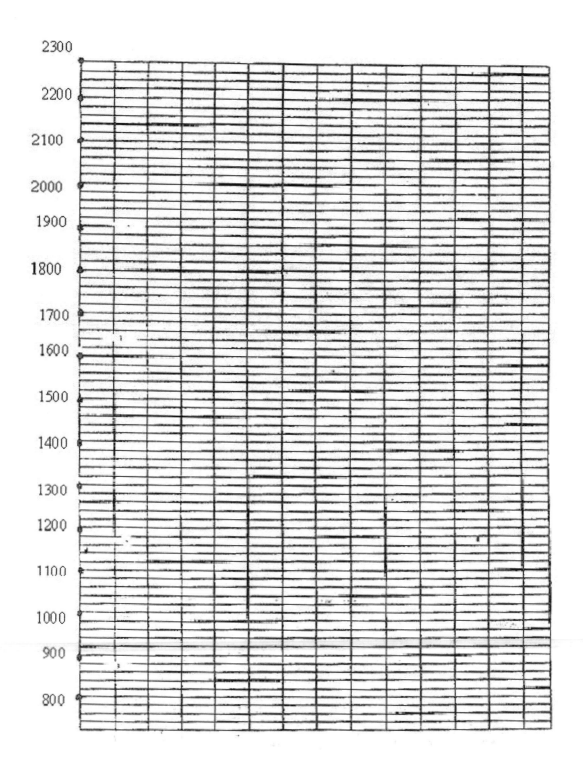

ORGANIZING YOUR CLIENT

An Organizing Project

Project Preparations

As mentioned in the previous chapter, an organizer may need to start off with a simple questionnaire or perform a Needs Assessment in order to ascertain the problems and recommend solutions. You might also need staff input to find out more about problem situations.

After assessing the "damages," write a Case Report and make a list of things that will need to be included in the project, in order of priority. With this evaluation you'll also be able to determine and recommend any organizing tools the client should purchase for the organizing project.

It is important for organizers to be aware of the various organizing products available in the marketplace. You'll develop creative solutions in helping a client get organized.

Before starting, ensure that the client agrees with the tasks that you recommend doing and how you plan to tackle them.

Supplies and Materials for a Project

In some cases, an organizer may need to come equipped with certain supplies for a project. For example, gloves protect hands and face masks protect your health in very dirty surroundings. It's always a good idea to have whatever supplies you feel you need to work on a particular project.

For example, if you know you are going to do a filing system, a good tool to have with you is a large file bin to sort files into as you re-classify (re-categorize) them.

Starting the Job

Starting the activities of a job project on the first day can vary from job to job. As already stated, an organizer will have a fairly good idea where to begin after an initial consultation.

Depending on the findings from the Questionnaire or Needs Assessment, an organizer may request the client's participation. In any decision-making segment, the client will need to be involved.

The client may need to understand however, that they are buying your professional expertise, as well as your time, and that working with you on the project is necessary in order to achieve the best results.

Overall, the organizer should plan to try to do as much as they can without using too much of the client's time, if possible. For example, the organizer can pre-sort papers or categorize items in a room while the client goes about their own business. When you're ready for the client's participation, this will be involving what to keep or what to get rid of.

Closing Time

Most often, the organizing project is done over days, even weeks. In the middle of it, the area you are working in probably has several messes created by you (disregarding the original mess it may have started out with!).

At the close of each organizing session (day), be sure to tidy up. That means, before you leave for the day, straighten up as best as you can to allow the client to operate in a happier environment. You may want to allow thirty minutes for a clean-up.

Close of a Project

When an organizing project is near or at an end, go over the areas and the systems you implemented with the client. See if there is anything else that needs to be done.

This may involve reassessing the new order. Ensure that the reorganization and new systems work for the client. Go over anything else you feel will help the client maintain order. Reiterate any of the key points you advised while educating them.

If you find that there is anything that needs to be tweaked, amend the system.

In reviewing the project, it provides closure and a sense of accomplishment of a job well carried out.

Client Reports

Occasionally, a client may wish to receive periodic reports on the organizing project, if extended over a long period of time. Here is a sample of one:

(DATE)

Client: (CLEINT NAME)

PROJECT REPORT
Re: Organization services for the home.

Hours used: _____ total

Work performed in (month) consisted of:

1)   Sorting and organizing desk area, papers, and filing system
2)   Sorting guest room papers into new filing system
3)   Organizing guest room and hall closets
4)   Organizing laundry room pantry
5)   Organizing kitchen-dinette cabinet shelves

Recommendations:

1)   Get file guides for filing system categories in one desk drawer

What's next:

1)   Finish sorting papers from kitchen area and guest room closet.
2)   Organize dining room closet shelves.
3)   Organize living room shelves (in entertainment unit).
4)   Label file folders (if desired).
5)   Consultation on paper flow and paper management.
6)   Consultation on categorizing and using computer directory "My Documents" to store all computer documents created (from any application).

Estimated hours left on project: 10

Prepared by:
(YOUR NAME)

Working with the Client

Some mistakes an organizer will make are in *asking* the client how they want something. Never do this. Give them suggestions and alternatives, but never ask them something that they paid for your expertise about.

It is a big blunder to put the client in a position of figuring out a solution. They will look upon you as an amateur and the project will go downhill from there.

In other words, you are the one who makes decisions on organizing solutions and they are the one who makes decisions on what they're keeping or letting go of.

Even if you recommend a solution that they don't agree with, it's better than not making a recommendation at all and asking for the client's opinion on what should be done. Remember, if your solution doesn't work for the client, just change it, and keep changing it until you find a system that works for that client.

Now, this is not to say that you don't ask the client certain questions in order to gather information. Of course we need to do that in order to provide good advice or make appropriate recommendations.

An organizer may also need to assist the client with decisions about items you feel they should get rid of. In this case, an organizer can ask questions about what value the item has to the person, helping them make a decision on whether to keep it or not.

Personality Types

People can be categorized into various "organizational" personalities by how they deal with situations relating to organization.

We're not talking about psychological conditions, behaviors, or traits. We're referring to characteristics that relate specifically to organization and how certain people deal with it, or don't deal with it.

An organizer can pretty much surmise the type of person they are dealing with as soon as they see the area or start a communication with the person. It's a simple observation, really.

Here are some to take notice of:

- The pack rat (AKA "the hoarder") - keeps everything and finds it difficult to let go of things.

- The procrastinator - puts things off, has a difficult time starting things, and waits until the last minute to take action.

- The slob - tends to be messy, and can't be bothered to put things away.

- The hider - keeps everything hidden away, out of sight.

- The viewer - keeps everything out in plain view to see, hates to put things away.

- The perfectionist - keeps everything tidy and wants things to be perfect (a "neat freak").

Then, there's "us" -- the ones who like to have things organized and don't take kindly to clutter in our own spaces. An organized person has certain characteristic traits that include:

- Putting things away in specified places
- Keeping a place for everything
- Using systems to function more efficiently
- Keeping appointments and arriving on time
- Remembering special events

These kinds of traits can be learned and developed. It may take longer for some people than others, but a person can change if given proper guidance and maybe some coaching.

Educating the Client

As consultants, we are as valuable as we can enlighten and educate our clients.

As you work with the client, let them know how to keep and maintain the order you're putting in. When you develop systems that help them maintain organization, ensure that they understand the system and have their agreement it can be easily maintained by them.

PRACTICAL IV-1:

Arrange to organize a family member or friend. It can be as simple as organizing one of their drawers to organizing their closet. It can even be consultation without implementation. The idea is to go through the motions of working with someone. Write up your results.

Working with Special Clients

ADD Clients

Professional Organizers will often come across clients with Attention Deficit Disorder (ADD) or Attention Deficit & Hyperactivity Disorder (ADHD). The reason is because these "type of people" are typically unable to focus easily and therefore become disorganized.

To give you a better understanding of clients diagnosed with this labeled "disease," I want to give you a little history on how this "illness" suddenly became so widespread, practically overnight, and then discuss methods in working with these types of clients.

Excerpts from an article by Fred A. Baughman Jr., MD, "*History of the Fraud of Biological Psychiatry*" that discuss the history of ADD as a "disease."

"In 1948, the combined specialty of 'neuropsychiatry' was divided into 'neurology,' dealing with organic or physical diseases of the brain, and 'psychiatry' dealing with emotional and behavioral problems in normal human beings."

"Psychiatry had already cast its lot with the pharmaceutical industry. By the late 1960's psychiatric drugs were 'big' business,' growing 'bigger.' "

"By 1970, it was apparent that psychiatry and the pharmaceutical industry had agreed upon a joint marketplace strategy: they would call psychiatric disorders, that is, all things emotional and behavioral, 'brain diseases' and would claim that each and every one was due to a 'chemical imbalance' of the brain. Further, they would launch a propaganda campaign, so intense and persistent that the public would soon believe in nothing but pills-- 'chemical balancers' for 'chemical imbalances'."

"Just as the National Institute of Mental Health (NIMH) is the primary author of the psychiatric condition/disorder-as-a-disease, deception, attention deficit hyperactivity disorder (ADHD) is their prototypical, most-successful-by-far, invented disease. They regularly revise its diagnostic criteria, not for any scientific purpose, but to cast a wider marketplace 'net.' "

"There were few claims by psychiatry in the sixties and seventies, of a biologic basis of psychiatric disorders, i.e., that they were "diseases." Such claims, without scientific evidence, began, in earnest, in the eighties and nineties, with the American Psychiatric Association's Diagnostic and Statistical Manual-III-R." ■

This article goes in an in-depth study and analysis and "exposé" of this type of diagnosis. The ADHD/Ritalin portion now stands at an estimated 6-7 million. There is a lot of documentation on the harmful effects of this drug and other amphetamines, but I won't get into it here.

In retrospect, there are people who diagnose themselves with a condition like ADD and don't take any pill for it. For those who suffer from symptoms of the condition, I will occasionally recommend natural alternatives that will help them overcome the symptoms. It is up to you, as an organizer, whether or not you want to propose such alternatives.

If you care to read up on it, you'll find information on this on the internet at:

- www.alternativementalhealth.com/articles/DrugfreeADD.htm
- www.healthxl.com/add.html

Now, let's look at how we can make a difference, as professional organizers, with people diagnosed with this condition.

Organizing Techniques for ADD Clients

As with any client, systems or methods of doing an activity need to be established to create organization. Some clients (like ADD clients), however, need a more disciplined system than others.

Each systemized approach will vary from individual to individual. It varies depending on the person's circumstances. For instance, if a person is always misplacing their keys, a system would need to be developed that gives them a place to put their keys when they arrive home.

Because we're the experts, the professionals who specialize in organization, we're capable of thinking of simple solutions that may be considered "so logical, why didn't they think of it?" Therefore, in analyzing a situation, don't assume they knew a solution but just didn't apply it.

In some cases it's true -- they knew a solution to handle a situation but didn't do anything about it. Your job would then be to consult with them in having a more disciplined and persistent approach in tackling their problem and developing new habits.

People who have difficulty focusing need proper nutrition (as this is often a nutrition issue, not a disorder) and simple methods in which to operate.

They may need to do activities in stages, or broken down into smaller parts, or segments of time. Whatever the case, work with the client in:

- Establishing methods in carrying out their activities
- Providing a place for everything
- Managing time and tasks

Our job is to steer them into a course of action that they can stick to in accomplishing their day with ease and get things done.

Although it may not seem that much different in establishing systems for a special client as it does with a typical client, the difference is that you may need to consider more unconventional methods for them.

Obsessive Disorders

The most common problem organizers will encounter with clients who are obsessive is hoarding, also referred to as Obsessive-Compulsive Disorder (OCD), also known as "pack rats." These individuals have certain things in common:

- They have difficulty processing information
- They have emotional attachments to possessions
- They avoid behavioral changes
- They have distorted beliefs on the importance of possessions
- They are indecisive

Each of these factors overlaps in various ways, affecting their ability on decision-making and organization.

This client has manufactured the idea that something very important is embodied in their possessions. With newspapers and magazines, it may be information. With junk mail, it may be opportunities. With miscellaneous items, it may be that they feel they will need it someday.

Here are some guidelines in working with this type of client:

- Because of their indecisiveness, all important aspects of each possession must be examined closely before discarding.

- Due to their inability to process information easily, define category boundaries more narrowly. Creating many categories may be required to classify possessions.

- To lessen worry that something will be forgotten if put away, start with putting things in piles to be sorted later and leaving it in sight.

- Since the idea of discarding possessions is too frightening, focus on decision-making training that involves category creation and moving designated possessions to storage.

Have many "excavation" sessions with homework between sessions. Work on restructuring their beliefs, behaviors, and emotional attachment to possessions.

Chronic Disorders

Chronic disorganization refers to the fact that the individual has been disorganized persistently and has a history of being disorganized for a long period of time.

> As Judith Kolberg says in her book, "*Conquering Chronic Disorganization*":
>
> *"Chronic disorganization is not a medical condition…But we have in mind here chronic disorganization as a quality of life issue, not a medical condition."*

Again, we're looking at a condition that should be treated as an issue, not a disease. This is all very good because we're not here to give them mental therapy, just organizing therapy.

An organizer should understand that using conventional organizing methods won't produce long-lasting effects on someone with chronic disorganization. They think and operate differently, so typical logic may not work on these individuals.

What needs to be addressed is the chronic aspect of their behavior. If you can determine the reason for a particular situation, you may devise a solution, albeit unusual. Kolberg's book has various solutions for dealing with these types of clients, so I won't attempt to provide tips and advice already covered in her book.

My purpose here is to make you aware of the various types of clients you may work with and how to approach each type. If you don't feel confident or experienced enough in working with these types of clients, it is best to refer them to someone who can.

MARKETING & PROMOTING YOUR BUSINESS

The Market

Targeting Your Public

In order to determine what public you want to target, make a list of groups who need organizing, in one way or another. Each group may have its own organizing needs and requirements for putting order into a disordered area. Your list might include:

ADD/ADHD individuals
Business owners
Business executives
Corporations
Entrepreneurs
Friends / Family
Home-based business
Homeowners
Housewives
Married with children
Mothers
Professionals
Retired individuals
Small companies

Each list can be broken down into sub-group categories. For example, professionals can be broken down into:

Accountants
Attorneys
Chiropractors
Consultants
Dentists
Doctors
Entertainment people
Insurance agents
Veterinarians
...and so on

People You Know

Many people starting out in a business make a list of people they know to publicize their new endeavor.

The U.S. Post Office has already prepared a general list of people to inform when you are moving and this "change of address booklet" might be a useful guideline for trying to remember everyone who could be contacted.

Just like you would send out a mailer to let others know you moved, you could send out a postcard or letter to your list of friends, family, associates, etc. letting them know about your new business.

Mailing Lists

As one grows their business, mailing lists can be purchased to help expand your market potential. In making targeted lists, you will find there is no end to people who need organizing services.

Study the demographics of your target public before acquiring any lists. Determine the best demographic profile, and go from there.

Target Demographics

A demographic profile of a home-based business is:

Title:	Business owner
Power:	Decision Maker
Viewpoint:	Big picture
Position:	Plans and strategies
Emotional influences:	Growth
Practical influences:	Efficiency
Education:	College degrees
Limitations:	Financial
Age:	35-65
Income:	$75,000-$750,000
Gender:	Male
Family:	Married with children
Geographic:	Suburban and urban
Occupation:	White collar, blue collar
Attitude:	Innovator

PRACTICE V-1:

Make a list of the markets you want to target.

Marketing Strategies

A Marketing Plan

Your Marketing Plan should state the plans for achieving an objective. From this, you will have direction for all the project activities within the overall plan.

The plan outlines all the actions you will need to do in order to accomplish your goals. Management cannot achieve successful results without a strategic plan, therefore planning is essential for success. One piece of advice: Never stop brain-storming for marketing ideas.

Here is a compilation of some marketing ideas:

- **Business cards**. Carry and post your business cards on bulletin boards or wherever you can!

- **Brochures.** Use brochures to describe your services or products, emphasizing the benefits.

- **Flyers.** Use flyers to promote a special service or special offer.

- **Newsletters.** Send out regular newsletters with informative tips and advice.

- **Postcards**. Send out postcards about a special offer, special event, or an organizing tip.

- **Press releases.** Send out press releases for news information or events.

- **Web sites**. With on-line marketing, you can publish informative tips and promote your services or products.

- **On-line Forums and news groups**. Enter on-line Forums or news group areas and post advice in your field of expertise.

- **Calendar Events.** Promote specials for "back to school," summer vacations/travel, tax preparations, spring cleaning, etc. Also, note special "organizing" events at the end of this chapter!

- **Event Participation.** Consider giving special offers to participants in a benefit and ensure you inform the media!

- **Networking.** Attending various groups or associations, conferences, chambers of commerce, is a powerful marketing method and helps build relationships. This is a means to promote your business and network among other comrades.

- **Local chambers** of commerce provide networking opportunities and support.

- ***Booths.*** Having a booth at an event or trade show is a great way to promote your services and/or products. One can get quite creative in putting together the materials to display at a booth. Flyers, brochures, "organizing tips" articles, your portfolio, published work, a giveaway prize for the first caller who wants to get organized, plus many other things to make your booth attractive, fun and interesting.

- ***Community involvement.*** Contributing to your community helps you gain recognition and exposure, as well as building relationships (i.e., Do you have a civic association you can belong to?).

- ***Special Interest Groups.*** If you have special interests, there is probably a group for it. Join and build relationships with other fellow members (i.e., a writer's association, a car club, a sewing group, an artist's society, etc.).

- ***Referral Programs.*** Ask satisfied clients for referrals. Offer an incentive, like a discount on future services or a commission (see "Building & Maintaining Clientele" in this chapter).

- ***Advertising.*** Place ads in local newspapers (see "Advertising & Promotion" in this chapter).

- ***Moving "Billboard."*** Some Organizers like to put a magnetic sign on their car and this may be something to consider.

- ***Company Tee-shirts.*** Wearing a tee-shirt displaying your company or product is a good way to get noticed! It may even strike up a conversation with someone.

There are many avenues in which to promote your business. As a writer uses the environment for ideas, a business person can do the same. See that ad on a roadside bench? How about that person sitting on a panel or at a booth giving advice? Or maybe that car traveling on the road that has a sign which makes you want to call? Just look around--there are many ways to get your message across.

International Organizing

Reprint of my article published in the NAPO National newsletter, Oct. 2001:

It's a big world out there. Nonetheless, with the growing number of NAPO members and new GC* veterans coming aboard, the world continues to stay as big as it's always been. What this means is, there is plenty of room for all of us, no matter how much we grow.

In observation of our industry's growth, many of us have expanded our services and/or products, much of which now spans to international levels (thanks to the Internet). Subsequently, the phrase: "Reach out and touch someone" takes on new significance when incorporated into our business practices on a global scale.

With nearly 1400 NAPO members currently, and approximately 4 billion people on the planet, it is clear there's plenty of business out there for each professional organizer, yes? It's what we do with our expertise and skills that bring in more business, therefore thinking "global" is an important factor.

So, how can we reach out internationally? Speakers, for one thing, are growing at exponential rates. If you aren't skilled in public speaking, there are many ways to learn how. For example, joining Toastmasters International will help you develop or hone your abilities. With this training, you could expand your repertoire of skills into various arenas around the world.

Workshops and seminars, or a lecture series, can be presented for small to large businesses, groups and associations. Also, Professional Organizers have become product spokespersons featured in media tours, and appearing on television around the world. The opportunities are endless in this field.

Another possibility is to write organizing books or booklets, or publish newsletters and E-Zines (electronic magazines). Therefore, it is a very good idea to sharpen your writing skills. As an author, your positioning as an expert in our field shoots off the graph, and you can build up global subscribers and international sales (again, thanks to the Internet).

The fact is, the more we write, the more we sell. The more we sell, the more income we produce. It's simple mathematics.

There are more ways Professional Organizers are increasing business and income by "going global." Coaching or training is yet another big market to tap. On the Internet, there are "e" businesses everywhere we look.

It is an electronic age we live in, so e-coaching is quite simple to accomplish. Just put up a web site, right? Right!

Another phrase I like is: "Just build it and they will come." So true. When we publish a web site, we should set goals for increasing the number of web visitors. Take advantage of linking your articles on the Internet and utilize various Internet marketing approaches. The more we put out there (build), the more people will come.

*GC - Golden Circle: comprised of organizers who have been in business for 5 years or more and a member of NAPO for 1 year.

It might also be a good idea to add other domain web sites for specialized services or products. These days, business on the Internet could produce as much income as local organizing services. Look at the trends and you'll see that people do make money on the Internet.

As we become more positioned as an expert in our field, the opportunities internationally become limitless. The first call I received to make a television appearance, I was naturally floored. How did they find me? The Internet. Then, other calls came in to appear doing TV segments, and I have the Internet and referrals to thank for that. Look at Julie Morgenstern, Barbara Hemphill and numerous other organizing veterans. They couldn't have set a better example for us. Just look at all they've accomplished. We all salute them for what they've done for our industry.

I only want to point out that we must learn what our potentials are and go after them furiously and, of course, globally. Simply consider the possibilities. ∎

PRACTICAL V-2. Make the following observations:

- *Observe other advertisements to get promo ideas.* Where do you see it? What is being promoted? How is it being said? What do you like/dislike about it?

- *Observe your environment to develop new strategies and plans.* Are there certain types of people and businesses which you want to do business with? Is a company re-locating? Down-sizing?

- *Observe other promotional and PR capers to spark public relations activity ideas.* Is someone sitting at a booth offering you a free taste of their food product? Did you read a newspaper article or watch a new segment on television about someone who did something interesting (and newsworthy)?

- *Observe what organizing articles are being written to make industry comparisons.* What was written? Where was it written? Who was featured?

- *Observe what is being written in business, marketing, or entrepreneurial magazine articles.* Is there useful information which would enhance an organizer's professional development? Do they offer good advice and spark interesting ideas?

- *Observe what other organizers are doing to expand your area of expertise and services*. Are they delivering workshops and seminars? Writing articles or books? Public speaking? Participating as an exhibitor at a convention? Selling products?

- *Observe how other organizers work together to form new alliances which produce recognition*. Did they work on a panel together? Do a job together? Participate in a news event together? Get on a NAPO committee? Co-write an article?

Advertising & Promotion

In promotion, think about what you want others to know. Try asking these questions:

- What is it that makes you and your service distinct from others?
- What do you offer and why would others want it?
- What are the benefits of your service?
- What does your public want that you can give them?

Writing Ad Copy

Consider what you want to communicate and, if writing copy for a flyer or display ad, pick one concept in which to write about. On the other hand, for putting together a brochure, you will, of course, need to provide as much information about your service(s) as possible.

I highly recommend some preliminary research by surveying to find out what your public needs. You will discover some useful information to include in your promotional endeavors. Although other Organizers may have researched to find out what to offer that their publics want, it is still a good idea to do your own.

Ad Sample:

Advertising Outlets

Print advertising is, of course, the less expensive medium in which to advertise, yet your local cable television company is something which can be considered later, if desired.

For placing a classified ad, I suggest looking into local newspapers in your area and/or areas in which you want to serve. These publications are usually less costly than the larger newspapers.

There may be some local or special directories that sell listings. For the entertainment industry, for example, there are several types of directories. Of course, if you have a business telephone line, you will be listed in the Yellow Pages. For this, talk to your phone company and ensure they place your company under "Organizing Services" or "Organizing Consultants."

It is a good idea to make up ad copy on 3 X 5 index cards to carry around with you (in your car or purse) so that these can be posted on bulletin boards. Posting your business card is another method. After all, this is free advertising and is a great outlet to promote your business.

Web Site Promotion

If you have a web site (and you should), there are many web promotional activities and opportunities you can partake in, such as:

- Keyword advertising
- Banner ads
- Links to site
- Strategic partnering
- Publishing articles on other sites (that link to yours)
- E-Zines (electronic magazines or newsletters) advertising
- Internet bulletin boards and news groups
- Affiliate Program
- Search engine and directory submissions
- Email marketing campaigns
- Web URL in letterhead stationary, business cards, signature lines

Hand-Outs

When starting out, it is not uncommon that business people "pound the pavement" and go door-to-door to hand out their flyer or brochure. I did! One can select certain office buildings or residential communities to distribute flyers or brochures. Or, one can hire a flyer distribution service to deliver in residential areas.

Promotional Mail-Outs

For the cost of printing and postage, regular mail outs are a must. Whether it's a letter (with brochure insert), a flyer or newsletter, this tells your public you're there and what you can do for them.

The reason it's good to send routine mailings to your public is because they will eventually, if not at first, call you when your message "hits them." If you've ever received regular flyers from a gardener, you probably threw them away until, one day when you needed one or wanted to change gardeners, it came to your door and you called him.

Email Marketing

Email marketing helps you keep in touch with clients and prospects electronically. It's a way of communicating much less expensively than with direct mail, saving money in printing and postage costs.

Here are some benefits with Email marketing:

- Generates an immediate response
- Maximizes reach, minimizes cost
- Increases traffic to Web site
- Reinforces the awareness of your brand in people's memories over longer time periods
- Response rate is better than traditional advertising - 3-15%

You can get more information about Email marketing at various Web sites, including: marketingprofs.com, gotmarketing.com, and roving.com.

When Business Slows Down

When business slows down, beef up your promotion going out -- even if finances are tight! If you're sending out 100 pieces a week by direct mail, send out 150-200 when income drops.

Also, get on the phone and start calling any leads that were interested, but never got started. Or leads who you've made contact with about an organizing project. Or, cold calls!

The key to slow business is more promotion.

PRACTICAL V-3:

Make a list of what promotional activities you want to do. Use this list to incorporate into your marketing plan section of your overall business plan.

Publicity

Publicity, unlike advertising, does not require payment for time or space. It is not public relations either, which is a broader task, yet includes publicity.

A Publicity Plan

Not everyone writes a publicity plan, however it is a good idea to do this if one wants to reach out to the media.

If you have a story with a slant or angle to communicate, submit a press release. If you don't know how to write a press release, NAPO-LA has prepared press releases in which an Organizer can use to send out to their local newspapers or other public sources.

Public relation firms keep a media book which is a compilation of media outlets (newspaper, radio, television) and contact names at each one.

One can begin to compile their own media book by researching their local media outlets and putting together categorized lists of them. With this, you can be your own public relations (PR) consultant.

Radio & TV

For anyone who feels comfortable in front of a camera and is able to communicate as an expert authority, there are radio and television talk shows to approach.

Workshops & Seminars

For anyone who feels comfortable in front of an audience of people and is able to communicate as an expert authority, they can deliver workshops or seminars on their organizing specialty.

Public Speaking

Making public speaking presentations will open many doors and help position you as an authority in your field. It may be better to have accomplished something first, or have a product which relates to that profession or industry (like a book, or articles, etc.), but this is not always necessary if you have confidence in your topic.

How-To Articles

If you enjoy writing, you can write "how to" articles and organizing tips for magazines and/or newspapers. This gives readers useful information which will bring about interest in you and your service.

<u>**PRACTICAL V-4**</u>:

Write a list of goals and objectives for your publicity efforts.

Making the Sale ⬅

Initial Contact

For initial contact, ask them:

1. What their organizing concerns and problems are.

2. What is the biggest problem area(s)?

Let them know you can help them put order into the area and that you use a systemized approach in dealing with problem areas, which creates an efficient environment they can operate in.

Follow-Ups

Don't "dance around" potential clients. If you haven't closed them in the initial contact, follow up to find out:

1. If they are still interested in putting their life in order -- see if their circumstances have changed.

2. What their initial motivation was in contacting you -- re-establish their goal and purpose.

3. How being organized would help them now -- have them see how getting organized would enable them to accomplish more things and have more time (go over the benefits again).

If they feel they should really postpone the project much longer -- have them see that it's better not to postpone this undertaking (it's usually what got them in trouble in the first place!). Take control and try to steer them into making a commitment on getting organized.

Don't give them choices on whether they want to want to start and when. Instead, give them choices such as:

- "What day is better for us to get started -- Monday or Tuesday? This week or next week?"

- "I have the end of next week available. How does that work for you?"

The idea in giving them choices is to get them to make a decision on WHEN, not IF they want to start.

Building & Maintaining Clientele

Building Clientele

It is good practice to implement a Referral Award Program, or some such program. This not only helps build your client base, but you'll usually have a built-in trust with the new client because of a mutual relationship.

Word-of-mouth is the best and most fruitful way of acquiring new business. Usually it comes after being in business for some time however, if your service is really great, you will begin to be referred to their friends and associates immediately.

Building Relationships

Relationship building can be done in many ways. Even a simple handwritten "thank you" note to a client (for their business) is appreciated.

It isn't always necessary to take a client to lunch, yet it does allow both of you to get to know one another better on a more personal level.

Here are some things you can do to build relationships:

- Send flowers or a gift basket (for a birthday).
- Call regularly and stay in touch with "How are things going?"
- Get your client's opinion about something, like from a survey question.
- Refer your client's service or product to other clients.

By staying in touch and caring about your client, they will want you back and, most likely, think of you as some other project comes into the picture.

You can provide special "Maintenance" offers to existing clients where they receive a discount on services for routine maintenance. Many of them want to buy hours "on credit" for this!

Some companies may even put you on their Organizing Board as an "Organizing Consultant" because you've planted the seed in their minds that they can call upon you anytime for guidance, troubleshooting, or just simple advice.

Strategic Partnerships

In growing your business to higher levels, partnering up with companies that compliment yours allows them to provide a value-added service, and strategic alliances can be formed.

Here is an example of the type of companies you can partner up with:

- Real estate agents
  - staging homes

- Convention meeting directors
  - organizing events

- Closet companies
  - organize closets

- Feng Shi consultants
  - de-clutter / organize homes & offices

- Interior decorators
  - organize homes & offices

- Accountants
  - organize finances

- Records Management consultants
  - organize files

- Insurance companies
  - insurance claims

- Product companies
  - sell organizing products

Partnering For Success

A reprint from my article, "Partnering For Success":

It's not a new concept, although it is becoming more popular among some fast growing businesses. This approach to "vertical selling," or cross-promotional marketing via partnering is known as strategic alliances.

Joining forces with other companies has proven to be a clever growth strategy in complementing existing products and services. When this kind of synergy is formed, the potential of doubling market penetration is strong.

Partnering is a close alliance and teaming up with others can boost your business. By integrating one's product or service with another, a collaboration of minds typically yields higher growth rates, larger revenues, greater productivity, and innovative ideas.

Small business owners looking for an "in" to large businesses could first approach a potential business partner with a letter describing what they have to offer them. This, of course, should be directed at a potential partner who has an equal amount to offer the partnership you desire. You would want a partner relationship that has resources and/or expertise you don't have. Partnering shouldn't be a fix for your problems. It's really a long-term visionary plan and, in view of the level of partnership desired, should aid in taking you to the next level of success.

Partnering with customers or clients is also an innovative move. This relationship provides a resource for business referrals. Same applies to partnering with suppliers, another helpful strategy for small businesses.

In building and/or enhancing your reputation, partnering with your community will produce more exposure and goodwill. This builds more relationships, thereby building business.

No marketing plan should exclude business development, and partnering with a complementary business may just be what you need. ■

Organizers Working Together

Reprinted from the Official Publication of the National Association of Professional Organizers, "NAPO News" Winter 1996 issue is an article written by myself and Donna McMillan:

"Together We Are Better" has been the philosophy of NAPO since its establishment eleven years ago. The five founding members had a vision and formed a support group of related services, those who organized their clients in one way or another. They welcomed a wide array of businesses and believed in the "Golden Rule." As publicity about professional organizers spread across the country, others joined their crusade, providing notable "validation" for our extraordinary careers.

Donna McMillan said, 'Like others, I had a dream to provide personalized services, utilizing my own diverse organizing skills, and felt a powerful yearning to build relationships with other business owners who would support and understand me. Most entrepreneurial friends were empathetic, but I truly found an unmatched kinship through NAPO (both locally and nationally), which is unique and invaluable.

'Because NAPO members come from distinctive background, specialties, interests, and lengths of experience, it is most advantageous to utilize others' products and services to care for our clients. Occasionally, prospects request services or products that I don't provide. By referring them to a colleague, or bringing one in on a project, the client is furnished high-quality service. They're also impressed that NAPO members are not competitors!'

'Initially,' said Cyndi Seidler, 'I didn't quite grasp the meaning of a particular statement made by Donna McMillan, then NAPO-LA president, at my first meeting. She pointed out that professional organizers should not feel competitive with one another, that we should be supportive and work together in building our careers and businesses. It wasn't until later that I fully understood how this worked. We are, after all, in the same business and typically a group of people who are all in the same profession feel competitive with one another, don't they? Well, I have come to learn that this is where professional organizers differ.

Instead of trying to covertly learn others strategies and marketing approaches to gain that competitive edge, we openly share our strategies, ideas and products. The words which state the purpose of NAPO are not just words, but actions which stand behind those words, especially the part which says, '....to provide support, education, and a networking forum...'

'Partnering' with other professional organizers and associate members has truly been beneficial for me," according to Donna. "These friendships have resulted in the sharing of products, organizing techniques and business tips. I'm most grateful for referrals of my own services and products to clients as well as to national publications, which as resulted in great publicity for NAPO as well. NAPO associate members and individual members are essential to my business, and I've promoted their products, 'linked' their web sites to mine and quoted many of them, which develops exposure and authenticity for all of us."

Cyndi relates,"Although I didn't see all the various ways to work with other organizers at first, it just seemed to come naturally when I adopted the attitude of being supportive toward my colleagues. So, when I developed and published my own web site, without a second thought, I began listing various colleagues' organizing products, knowing this would be beneficial to the visitors at my site. Soon after, to my astonishment, the deed came back to me in ways I didn't calculate -- other NAPO members linked my products on their web sites. The result: additional orders."

Both Donna and Cyndi write articles and publish quarterly newsletters, where it is now par for the course to include a quote from another organizer or associate member. This not only makes their work more substantiated, but more informative and interesting. All these "little" things have culminated in business growth and prosperity, not to mention the good feeling it brings to be reciprocated with the kind of support and sharing that follows when you have things in proper perspective.

Cyndi summarizes by saying, "I have come to appreciate NAPO far beyond my initial expectations and I see now the true meaning of the old saying, "You get back what you put into something." ∎

PRACTICAL V-5.

Observe successful attitudes and practices. Listen to a motivational tape. Read a leadership article. Talk to someone successful and ask them how they got there.

Calendar of Special Organizing Events

January (2nd Mon. of month)	Clean Off Your Desk Day
January	Clean Out Your Closet Month
February	National Archive Your Files Month
February	National Time Management Month
February (2nd Mon. of month)	Clean Out Your Computer Day
March	National Get Ready For Tax Time Month
March (2nd Tue. of month)	National Organize Your Home Office Day
March (3rd week of month)	National Clean Out Your Closet Week
March (4th week of month)	National Clutter Awareness Week
April	National Tackle Your Clutter Month
April (3rd week of month)	National Organize Your Files Week
May	Revise Your Work Schedule Month
June	Rebuild Your Life Month
July (2nd week of month)	Take Charge of Your Life Week
August (1st week of month)	Simplify Your Life Week
September	Self-Improvement Month
September (2nd Thu. of mo.)	Do-It-Day (AKA Fight Procrastination Day)
October	Clean Out Your Files Month
October (2nd week of month)	Get Organized Week
October (3rd week of month)	Home-based Business Week
October (3rd week of month)	Evaluate Your Life Day
October (4th week of month)	Make A Difference Day
November	Get Organized For The Holidays Month
November	Clean Out Your Refrigerator Month
November	International Creative Month
December	Stress-free Family Holidays Month

EPILOGUE

A MANUAL FOR PROFESSIONAL ORGANIZERS

Paving the Road

With the information in this manual, you should now be ready to map your route and pave the road to a new career direction. Establishing a new business begins with some basic plans that lay the foundation. Building a business continues as you put the blocks together to make a solid enterprise for yourself.

Your path to a successful organizing business is ready to be paved with solid ambition. You now have enough sign posts to direct you along the way and your organizing colleges will be there to assist you in any way possible.

You are not alone in this profession. Go to local NAPO chapter meetings, attend NAPO conference, get a coach or mentor. There is a lot of support for you available and a lot of growth potential.

Remember, this field is wide open to anyone's creativity. The rewards in this business will bring fun and fulfillment to you and everyone you serve.

Set your goals and objectives, decide on your plan of action to arrive at your goal, and do those activities which get you there.

I wish you the best of happiness in your new business life.

> The future belongs to those who believe in the beauty of their dreams.
> --Eleanor Roosevelt

REFERENCES

Recommended Reading

On organizing.

BEST ORGANIZING TIPS
By Stephanie Winston, Simon & Schuster

CLEAN UP YOUR ACT
By Dianna Booker

CLUTTER FREE
By Don Aslett

CONQUERING THE PAPER PILE-UP
By Stephanie Culp

GETTING ORGANIZED
By Stephanie Winston, Warner Books

GETTING THINGS DONE
By Edwin Bliss

HOW TO LIVE THOUGH AN EXECUTIVE
By L. Ron Hubbard, Bridge Publications

HOW TO GET ORGANIZED WHEN YOU DON'T HAVE THE TIME
By Stephanie Culp

HOW TO ORGANIZE YOUR WORK & YOUR LIFE
By Robert Moskowitz, Doubleday

IDIOTS GUIDE TO ORGANIZING YOUR LIFE
By Georgene Lockwood, Alpha Books

THE OFFICE CLUTTER CURE
By Don Aslett, Marsh Creek Press

THE ORGANIZATION MAP
By Pam McClellan, Better Way Books

THE ORGANIZED EXECUTIVE
By Stephanie Winston, Norton & Company

ORGANIZE YOUR OFFICE!
By Ronni Eisenberg with Kate Kelly, Hyperion

ORGANIZED TO BE THE BEST
By Susan Silver, Adams Hall

ORGANIZING FOR THE CREATIVE PERSON
By Dorothy Lehmkuhl & Dolore Cotter Lamping,
Crown Trade Books

ORGANIZING FROM THE INSIDE OUT
By Julie Morgenstern, Owl Books

STREAMLINING YOUR LIFE
By Stephanie Culp, Writer's Digest Books

TAMING THE PAPER TIGER
By Barbara Hemphill, Kiplinger's Books

TAMING THE OFFICE TIGER
By Barbara Hemphill, Kiplinger's Books

On business.

BUSINESS PLAN GUIDE, The Ernst & Young
John Wiley & Sons, Inc.

EVERYTHING I NEEDED TO KNOW ABOUT
BUSINESS I LEARNED IN THE BARNYARD
By Don Aslett

GROWING A BUSINESS
By Paul Hawken, Simon & Schuster

STARTING YOUR OWN BUSINESS
By Stephen C. Harper, McGraw-Hill

STRATEGY
Harvard Business Review, HBS Press

On Marketing

GUERRILLA MARKETING
By Jay Conrad Levinson, Houghton & Mifflin

THE MARKETING IMAGINATION
By Theodore Levitt, The Free Press

On publicity.

MARKETING WARFARE
By Al Ries & Jack Trout, Plume Books

NEW DIRECTIONS IN MARKETING
By Aubrey Wilson, NTC Business Books

DO-IT-YOURSELF PUBLICITY
By David Ramacitti, Amacon

THE PUBLICITY HANDBOOK
By David Yale, NTC Business Books

WRITER'S GUIDE TO SELF-PROMOTION &
PUBLICITY
By Elane Feldman

Computer Software Organizers

ACCESS - a relational database that tracks sales figures, invoices, inventory, and personal information.

ACT 1 - a powerful contact management program.

ASCEND - a scheduler, task management, contact and information program (based on the Quest Franklin Planner).

CLARIS ORGANIZER - a popular PIM, with ability to launch web sites from within Organizer.

DAYTIMER - a scheduler and task management program

FILEMAKER PRO - a powerful database for information management.

FILEWISE DELUXE - a comprehensive document management software that organizes and tracks documents and information.

GOLDMINE - a contact management program.

LEADCOMMANDER - a contact management program "aimed at building relationships." Also contains to do lists.

LOTUS ORGANIZER - task management with a day-runner, calendar, contacts, to do lists.

MANAGE PRO - helps organize your projects and keeps track of their progress (specific use for human resources).

PAPERMASTER - stores document pages (needs scanner), acting as a personal file cabinet for documents.

GLOSSARY

Contact Management	A procedure for managing contacts, either electronically or manually. It is a method of keeping information on people and tracking all activities and tasks connected to them.
Document Management	The ability to store and retrieve documents in a centralized facility that is accessible to all. It is the managing of electronic files, graphics, images, and other data types used in document creation. A single document's files may contain text, charts, voice and video clips, process steps, fonts, and more. Document Management systems is the process which helps you keep track of stored documents that have been scanned into the computer or created by word-processing or Computer Application Devices (CAD) applications.
File Management	A system for managing files that usually involves organizing and tracking paper files stored in file cabinets.
Information Management	Information is an asset to an organization and the management of this information is a means to manage a document during its entire life cycle. The ability to know what documents exist regarding a particular subject, where they are located, what media they are stored on, who owns them, and when they should be destroyed. Information management encompasses document management, records management, imaging, and knowledge management systems.
Imaging Management	Similar to Document Management, this controls all media types used in creating and storing a document, whether scanned into the computer, downloaded from the internet, or created in a computer application.

Paper Management	Manages the flow of paper, from the moment it arrives on your desktop to the moment it is complete and/or goes out (either filed, stored, or discarded). Unlike Document Management which is an automated system that deals with electronic media, Paper Management handles or controls hard copy (printed) paper.
Project Management	Manages the production of projects with schedules and tasks associated with the project. It often involves detailed expertise in many of the following areas: planning, cost management, contract negotiations/procurement, technical writing (proposals, etc.), research, technical development, information/computer management, business development, corporate/administrative management, time management, and others. A Project Manager should have leadership as opposed to management skills, with well developed analytical skills.
Records Management	A means to manage a document during its entire life cycle. It controls the recorded information that is required for the continuance or recovery of an organization's business. Such control is exercised over the creation, distribution, usage, retention, and final disposition of all types of records within an organization, according to rules and constraints stated in laws and industry policies. The records management task is performed by classifying each document, uniformly, as to its subject, type, retention period, etc., and then storing the document's meta data in a database. Document meta data (information about a document. For example, the document's title, author, date of creation, location, media, classification, etc.) consists of the document's identification, storage location, media, media supported software (file extension), and other information.

Retention Schedules	A statement of when documents should be archived and destroyed based upon their subject matter, laws, industry standards, and corporate policy. There are some 1800 citations in the United States Code of Federal Regulations and various state codes that describe the legal retention of documents. The laws of other countries are similarly complex. These descriptions are only referred to by subject. As a result, the management of information assets must meet rigorous conditions to effectively comply with legal requirements. Retention schedules are usually associated only with the Records Management function and must be rigorously followed. A source of protection, and limiting exposure relating to litigation cases with the court, lies within a disciplined records management program and enforcement of records retention policies covering all media.
Task Management	This involves managing tasks, including project tasks. Keeping "to do" lists is one method of managing tasks. Tasks can also be managed electronically, often found in some computer applications that specialize in contact management.
Time Management	The ability to manage and control time. The use of planners, calendars, and the like are effective tools in managing time. Implementing a routine is a method of scheduling actions which enforce a regiment to fit with a person's flow of work and production activities.
Work Management	This consists of various systems to manage work and the flow of work (manually, as opposed to workflow which coordinates the flow of work electronically -- see definition below).

Workflow Management

It is a proactive computer system that manages and coordinates the flow of work (electronically) among participants, according to a procedure consisting of a number of tasks. It coordinates user and system participants, together with the appropriate data resources, which may be accessible directly by the system or off-line, to achieve defined objectives by set deadlines. The coordination involves passing tasks from participant to participant in correct sequence, ensuring that all fulfill required contributions. Workflow Management provides a set of functions that allow customers to define, validate, execute, manage, and reassess their business processes in an automated way. These business processes can be any line-of-business activities. For example, contacting for a purchase, the processing of an insurance claim, managing a lawsuit from start to finish, the steps in application development, or an enterprise-wide management function (such as installing a software update).

About the Author

"Organizer to the Stars" Cyndi Seidler is a leader in her field and has achieved international recognition as a Professional Organizer. She is often featured as an "Organizing Expert" on various popular radio programs, national television shows, magazines and local newspapers.

Over the years, Cyndi has made many noteworthy appearances on television shows including regular spots on HGTV's *Smart Solutions* for two seasons. Her DVD *"Get Organized with Cyndi Seidler"* is distributed at major retailers nationwide.

As an author, columnist, organizing consultant, speaker, spokesperson, and TV host, Cyndi's diversified talents have made her a popular figure among the organizing industry.

Cyndi appeared in TV media tours throughout the U.S. as a spokesperson for *Tupperware, Post-it Notes*, and *Quicken*, providing organizing tips and advice on morning news shows in key cities.

As a radio personality, Cyndi produced and hosted "*Organized Living With Cyndi Seidler"* on KIEV-870 AM (in 1999).

Cyndi's weekly syndicated column "*Organized Living*" runs in various newspaper publications, and her articles have been published throughout the country and on the internet.

Cyndi's books include, "*Organize for Success,*" "*The Art of Filing Systems,*" and "*A Manual for Professional Organizers*."

Founder/owner of *HandyGirl Organizers*, a Los Angeles based company; Cyndi has helped many individuals get organized. Since 1994, she has created and implemented organizing systems for homes and business. Her methods have helped prominent celebrities such as Sinbad, Eric Roberts, Karen Black, Tisha Campbell, Mary Lynn Rajskub, Larina Adamson, Bobbi Billard, Billy Sheehan, and Spencer Davis get a grip on their hectic lifestyles.

Her company Web site is at www.handygirl.com and personal web site is at www.cyndiseidler.com. She created the web site: www.organized-living.com.

Made in the USA